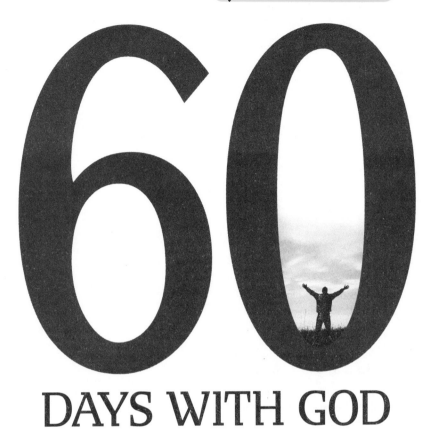

60

DAYS WITH GOD

DRAWING NEAR TO GOD
THROUGH TIMES OF CRISIS

Barry A. Wood

Deep River
B O O K S

Published by
Deep River Books
Sisters, Oregon
http://www.deepriverbooks.com

ISBN: 1-935265-76-8
ISBN 13: 978-1-935265-76-4

Library of Congress Control Number: 2011932211

Printed in the USA

Cover and interior design by Robin Black, www.blackbirdcreative.biz

TABLE OF CONTENTS

INTRODUCTION

There are many different kinds of crisis. Maybe you have lost a loved one. Perhaps you have had a major financial setback. Maybe you have serious health issues or have been diagnosed with a disease. You may have gone through a divorce or faced a broken relationship. Crisis comes in different forms, but the devastation to our lives is just as real no matter what the situation.

As Christians, we are not immune to crisis. Throughout the Bible, we see many times that crisis affected individuals, families, and nations. Whether it was a national crisis or a family crisis, it always affected people. In the book of Genesis, Joseph faced many crisis times. He was abandoned and left for dead at the hands of his brothers. He was falsely accused, thrown in prison, and forgotten there by those he helped.

King David faced many crises in his life. He was hated and pursued by Saul. This caused him to live his life on the run, despised by many as a fugitive. He was driven from Jerusalem by his own son. Perhaps the biggest crisis in David's life came as a result of his own actions. He fell into sin by lusting after Bathsheba, having an affair with her, and later having her husband killed. As a result of this sin, David felt the guilt and shame of his actions. Later, he was forced to deal with the death of his son who had been conceived through his sin with Bathsheba.

Whether crisis comes as a result of our own actions or through circumstances that are completely out of our control, the devastation and sense of loss is painful. There is a grieving process that takes place; a time of upheaval in our lives. There are two ways we can choose to deal with the effects of crisis. We either run to God or run away from him.

God's position in our lives remains constant. He is always there waiting to affect our lives with his love, compassion and care. It is our response to him that dictates the outcome of our crisis times. James 4:8 says, *"Draw near to God and He will draw near to you"* (NKJV). Logic would tell us that the opposite is also true. If we choose to run from God, he will be distant from us. The reality is: God has not gone anywhere. He remains there waiting. In fact, he wants to draw near to us. If we choose to draw near, he is right there ready to receive us. If we choose to run, he is still right there waiting for us to return. We must make the choice. My sincere hope is that when you face crisis, you will make the choice to run to God.

I have seven grandchildren, five years old and younger. Since my two daughters and their husbands and my son and his wife all live within a few minutes of our house, having the grandkids over is a regular occurrence. Not long ago, the Lord showed me a picture of himself and his relationship to me. When one of the grandkids comes over, they may run through the door and make a beeline for Grandpa. When I see them coming, my arms are open wide to receive them, pick them up, and hug and kiss them. Sometimes they come in the house and are timid. They don't run to me. They may stay back and just watch me to see what I will do. Even then, I open my arms and invite them to come to Grandpa. This is exactly the way God relates to you and me. When we run to him, he is waiting to receive us. He desires for us to come and leap into his arms. Even if we are timid and do not run to him, he is still there, arms open wide, ready to receive us.

God wants to guide us through times of crisis and bring us out the other end with new love for him, strength to go on, and power to live our lives effectively for him. How will we respond? Will we run to him? Will we stand timidly away from him pondering what our next move will be? Will we run away from him? Let me assure you:

God never changes! Hebrews 13:8 tells us, *"Jesus Christ is the same yesterday, and today and forever."* He is not changing. He is not leaving. He is not hiding. He waits for us to draw near to him so that he may draw near to us and bring us through times of difficulty and crisis.

Not long ago, I faced a crisis in my own life. After nine years at my job managing a distribution company, I was abruptly fired. There was no warning, no opportunity for dialogue. One day I had a job, was secure in my position, and doing well financially. The next day I was unemployed, in my fifties, with no idea what I would do next. I felt as if I had lost my worth. My job was lost and no other companies seemed to have a use for me. My world seemed to come crashing down around me. I know that many people have faced far more devastating things than this. But crisis is crisis. To me, this was big. It shook me to the core.

I was faced with the choice: Would I run to God or would I run away from him? I have walked with the Lord since I was seventeen years old. I have walked through good times and bad times with him. I knew him and I thought I knew him well. But in those first moments (after my firing), all of that didn't seem to matter. This was now. This was a time of crisis. This was a faith-shaking time.

It didn't take long, really, for me to make my decision. I knew in my heart that there were no other options. I could not run, for I have tried that before, to no avail. I could not hide, because I knew he would see me. I could not continue in my own strength, because I had none. I made a decision that day to draw near to God. That decision launched me into the journey of a lifetime. This was the kind of journey that changes lives, and it certainly changed mine.

I began to write my thoughts about this journey that very day. It didn't take long for me to realize that God not only was there to help through this time of crisis, his intent was to speak to me, change me from the inside out, and send me into new adventures with his purpose for my life. I found that each day the Holy Spirit was there to comfort and direct me in the new things that were in store that day. In all my life, there has never been such an intense time of learning and growing in my relationship with Jesus.

All of the content in the following pages was inspired by the journal I kept during the first sixty days of my struggle. In the months that followed, I learned much more as the Holy Spirit built on the foundation he had laid during this time.

In the chapters that follow, I invite you to take that journey with me as I share with you all that God did and said through my *Sixty Days with God*. Each chapter is titled with a word of promise from the Holy Spirit. Each one of these things changed my life. My desire is that somehow through the words written here, you will see that through your time of crisis, God is right there with you. His desire is not only to help you through your difficult time, it is to change and equip you to "finish the race" and to finish strong. His passion for us is to see us grow in our desire for him. When that passionate relationship is developed, you and I will never be the same.

1

"I AM ALWAYS WITH YOU"

The Need

*"The LORD himself goes before you and will be with you; he
will never leave you nor forsake you.
Do not be afraid; do not be discouraged."*

DEUTERONOMY 31:8

Tuesday mornings were always about the same. I was up early as usual and on my way to my work. I was the manager of a distribution company. Due to the national economic downturn, our industry had been struggling and sales were very poor. Each day was a challenge due to the fact that we were always in need of cutting costs in an effort to keep pace with the slowing sales market. I knew the success of our company depended on our ability to reduce costs enough to counter the lack of income. This particular Tuesday was the beginning of a new journey, one that would change my life forever.

I arrived at work and went to my office. My morning routine was to log into my computer and begin my duties. A coworker from another division of the company came in and told me the company president wanted to see me. It was unusual for him to be in his office that early in the morning. I didn't give it much thought as I walked across the parking lot to his office. A short time later, I left his office with my final paycheck in hand. I had been terminated.

I had never been fired from a job in my life. I had always had a good work ethic and took pride in my ability to get things done. But all of that meant nothing right now. This was not just the loss of a job; this was a devastation that shook the foundations of my life. My self-worth was attacked, my value was in question. My value as a provider and leader seemed to be lost along with my career.

I was numb as I drove home that day. Although I had been a Christian for many years, no prayers came to my mind. There were no thoughts telling me that this was just another step in my life. I could not reassure myself that everything was going to be okay. It seemed like an ending, not a beginning.

When I arrived home, I was greeted by my wife and best friend, Cathy. She was surprised to see me. This was a moment of dread. I had to tell her what had happened. Through tears, I told her about the events of the day. I told her I was fired and shared my feelings that my life was over. Does that sound dramatic? After all, this was just a job; no one had died. Disaster had not befallen our family. It was simply the loss of a job. But to me, it was more than that. It was a loss of part of me. I had found a sense of purpose in that job. It was a major part of my identity. And now it was gone.

The rest of that day, all my thoughts could be summarized as this, "What do I do now?" Those thoughts were on my mind as I left that afternoon to walk and pray. In my life, in times of trouble, it is therapeutic to walk and spend time with God. But I didn't have anything to pray. I had no faith, and I was gripped with an overwhelming sense of hopelessness. I felt alone. No scriptures came to my mind to comfort me. What would I do? What could I do?

It was while I was walking that one of the most profound truths of my relationship with God was revealed to me. The Holy Spirit, in his gentle and quiet voice, said to me; *"You know I am always with you."* I cried as I thanked him for reminding me of that reality. Although I had always believed that, it had a new meaning right then. It was the kind of experience that you can't really explain to others. It was a moment when God put his arm around me and took time just for me. He gave me a new perspective:

SOUND THE TRUMPET

"If the trumpet does not sound a clear call,
who will get ready for battle?"

1 CORINTHIANS 14:8

I had been teaching a class at our church called, "Standing in The Gap." It was a study in prayer and spiritual warfare. The day after my crisis began was to be the last session in the class. After a long night and another day of facing this circumstance, I had little desire to teach. I told Cathy that I wasn't going to teach that day. She asked me to pray about it and see if the Lord would want me to go. I don't actually remember the prayer, but I did take time to relax and try to escape from the pain. In a moment, I heard the Lord speak again, *"Barry, do you trust these people to do what they are being equipped to do and pray for you?"* I was forced to give an answer. The answer was yes. I did trust them to pray for me.

I did teach that night. I will never forget the subject for that class. It was "The Sounding of the Trumpet." In Old Testament times, the trumpet was sounded to gather people for a specific purpose. In the book of Nehemiah, they blew the trumpet to gather the people who were working on the rebuilding of the walls of Jerusalem. Wherever the trumpet sound was heard, there the people gathered to fight against the enemies who would come against the rebuilding of the city. The trumpet was blown to sound an alarm (Joel 2:1), to declare a holy fast (Joel 2:15), and to sound a battle cry (2 Chronicles 13:12). This was my time to sound the trumpet.

That night, people prayed for me. They laid their hands on me and asked God to help me in my time of need. They prayed for my wife and me to experience God in new ways through this time of crisis.

They cried with me, shared words of encouragement, and blessed my life with their sincerity of heart and their love and concern for us. They declared a day of fasting for us. It was just what I needed. I will never again doubt the wisdom of "sounding the trumpet" in times of need. God had placed me in a family, a family of believers who loved and cared for me.

I talked to my pastor. Like all good counselors, he listened to me as I shared my story through tears. I was in pain and he knew it. He didn't try to give me advice or direction. He simply listened, shared some encouragement with me, and prayed. I knew there was great value in seeking counsel from godly men, especially those who were placed as shepherds in my life.

In those early days of my crisis, Cathy was a great strength to me. There were many days when I didn't want to get out of bed and face the day. She was the one who encouraged me, prayed for me, and helped carry me through these difficult days. God was faithful to bless me with a partner who could strengthen me in my great time of need. When I felt alone, she was always there encouraging and loving me. God was expressing his love to me through people.

A Servant Comes

"After we had been there a number of days, a prophet came . . ."
ACTS 21:10

I hadn't seen John for eighteen years. He was my pastor in the early 1990's and had moved to a different part of the country. We talked on the phone once or twice and emailed a few times. So I was surprised when the phone rang and I saw his name on the caller I.D. He said, "If we were to come through your town tomorrow, would you be up for a visit?" This man had always been able to read me like a book. I have never had a friend who could speak the words of God into my life like he could. Of course we wanted to see him.

I must admit I felt a little like the lowly homesteader in a Hollywood western movie. I imagined the mysterious stranger riding into town through a foggy mist. The homesteader was always uncertain whether the stranger was a good guy or a killer coming to deal him the final blow. But this was different. God had a plan. He arranged this time just for us. From out of our past came a friend who loved us. He was bearing the very words of God for our time of crisis.

There was no small talk, no "How's the weather in your part of the country?" John and his wife, Carol, were here to do God's will. They sat down and asked, "What's going on?" It was as if there had been little time since we saw them last. Again, through tears, I told them what had happened and all the deep feelings of guilt, shame, and betrayal in me. They listened and in his usual soft-spoken and gentle voice, he asked, "Dear Ones, may we pray for you?" I had forgotten that he always called people "Dear Ones". This time, it was as if Jesus himself were speaking those words to us. We were receiving something that a man could not give. We were being touched by the Holy Spirit.

As John and Carol prayed for me, there was a great spiritual release. I could sense things in my life were being torn down by God. His intent was to rebuild me. In order to rebuild, some things in my life had to fall. They prayed for Cathy. Once again, it cut through all the surface issues and spoke to the root of what the Holy Spirit wanted to accomplish in her. We were refreshed that day. Healing had begun in our broken lives. All this on the very day my class had chosen to fast for us.

God is Faithful

"He who has begun a good work in you will complete it until the day of Jesus Christ."
Philippians 1:6 NKJV

It is impossible to convey through words the deep things God did for us in those first four days of our crisis. Something big had begun.

Although it was difficult to see at the time, God had a plan for this crisis time. His intentions were to build something great out of lives that were broken down. He was incredibly faithful. We needed him desperately and he was there to receive us and comfort us.

When I heard the Lord whisper to me that first day, *"You know I'm always with you,"* it set the tone for my restoration. They were simple words, ones that I have heard people say many times. I have heard teachers tell the congregation that God is with them always. I've read it in my Bible. But when God put his arms around me and spoke those words into my heart, I knew they were true.

SOME WORDS FOR YOU

The most important thing you will ever do in your crisis time is run to Jesus. There were many times when I said, "I don't know how people can make it through times like this without Jesus." It is absolutely true. He will always be there to draw near to you as you draw near to him.

Some people do not run toward God. They choose to run away. I have seen many Christians make choices to run. Often they end up falling into old habits or addictions. You see, in times of crisis, everyone needs someone or something on which to depend. It may be a person. It could be things. People may even attempt to find some "inner strength." Some find themselves slipping into drug or alcohol abuse. All of these things may soothe the pain for a time, but they will never bring you through your struggle with life-changing results. Only God can take a time of crisis and use it to build the rest of your life.

Even if you have made a choice to run from God, it is never too late to turn around and run to him. I love the story of the Prodigal Son; he made some poor choices and ran from his father. Although the time away began with a bang, he soon found himself in a deeply painful time. His circumstance was horrific. He reasoned that a trip home couldn't be worse than the place where he was, so he chose to run home to his father. Even if he became one of his father's servants, it would be a better life than he was experiencing. But when he arrived home, he found a father who ran toward him, clothed him with the best he could offer, and embraced him as his own son. You see, you can always run to your Father. God never changes and he will never disown you. He is waiting, in fact longing, for your return.

Once you have chosen to run to God, gather support. Find people who will stand with you. This is not to say that you should depend on people. You should depend on God and allow him to use people to touch your life. The same God who says, *"I am always with you,"* is fully able to bring people into your life who will pray and support you. I found that God supernaturally brought people to me to pray and speak words of encouragement. They shared things that gave me direction in my pursuit of God and his will for me. Christian people belong to God. He will use them to touch your life.

You will need to "sound the trumpet." If you have a family or a church family, call them and share your need. If you do not have either, find a church that teaches the Word of God and loves people. Many times, we feel that we should bear our burdens alone. But God never intended that for us. He is there to help us, and he has placed people in our lives to help us through struggles. Sound an alarm by sharing your needs with people you can trust. Once again, God will meet you.

Know that God is faithful. You are in a time of crisis that God wants to use to change your life. His desire is to lead you into things that you never thought possible. His purpose is always to perfect us. Start to view your crisis time as a blessing and not a curse. See it as a time to increase your relationship with God, to restore your love and commitment to him. You can be sure of this; God is faithful and he will complete what he has started in you!

2

"1 WILL STRENGTHEN YOU"

Practicing the Word

"Thy word is a lamp unto my feet, and a light unto my path"
PSALM 119:105 KJV

The battle had begun. In my entire Christian life, I have never experienced spiritual warfare like I did in those days. I fought battles daily, in fact, many times per day. I truly discovered that spiritual warfare takes place primarily in the mind. I began having what I later would call, "destructive thoughts." These were all-consuming thoughts of impending doom and destruction. I would think of financial calamity. I had many self-destructive thoughts as I looked back on my nine-year career in my job. I continually pondered what I could have done better or differently. Over and over again, I told myself it was all my fault. I was simply going to reap destruction.

It didn't take long for me to realize that those thoughts were planted by the enemy. When thoughts of destruction came, I would get physically ill. My heart would race. I dealt with uncontrollable chills and shaking. I wasn't eating properly. Everything seemed to be heading downhill quickly. I realized that all of these things were not God's desire for me. They were the attempts of the enemy to destroy me.

Faith began to rise in me. I thought, *if Satan is this bent on destroying me, God must have something great planned.* I decided the answers were in

God's Word. How could I fight these thoughts and come away victorious? I applied a passage of scripture that had always been important to me:

> *The weapons we fight with are not the weapons of the world. On the contrary, they have divine power to demolish strongholds. We demolish strongholds and every pretension that sets itself up against the knowledge of God, **and we take captive every thought to make it obedient to Christ.***
>
> 2 CORINTHIANS 10:4-5 (EMPHASIS MINE)

That was the answer! I had weapons to fight against those thoughts. I knew when they came. I could feel them throughout my whole being. So why not fight against them using this scripture passage? I love the simplicity of the words here. These weapons are not magical, they are not mystical. They are simple and available for use. The answer was: Take those thoughts captive and make them obedient to Christ.

When I woke up each morning, I was praying. Knowing that I had to face another day was enough to cause me to seek God. When the destructive thoughts came, I prayed. I simply said, "Lord Jesus, I take this thought captive. I want to make it obedient to you." It worked! Every time I had a thought, I would stop, pray, take it captive and move on. In those days, the thoughts were many. I applied this scripture numerous times each day to overcome in this battle in my mind.

This may not seem like a very profound discovery. But to me, this was like manna from heaven. I stood on this scripture. I used it. I quoted it all the time. Every time the thoughts came, I caught them, captured them. The simple prayer I prayed each time completed the battle for that thought. I was making my thoughts become obedient to Christ. Even though I was still dealing with the thoughts, I found peace in applying God's Word in every situation. I learned something that was changing my thought patterns. God was bringing his peace through the discovery of applying his Word in a simple way.

SEEKING HIS POWER

"Finally, be strong in the Lord and in his mighty power."

EPHESIANS 6:10

I found that God's Word was a true source of strength for me. This was a time when I had very little strength of my own. I needed God to be my strength. As I searched his Word for answers, I found something that would change my daily life forever. I was still dealing with a tremendous battle in my mind. What if I could attack those thoughts **before** they came? Was it possible to gain victory over destructive thoughts before I was in the heat of battle? There was an answer. There was a battle plan already laid out for me. All I had to do was appropriate it to my life.

In Ephesians 6, the apostle Paul gives very explicit instructions about how to seek God's power. The first thing I had to understand was: My source of strength is found in him, not me. I could do everything I could to try to overcome my circumstances. I could make attempts to solve the situation the best way I knew how. In fact, I had tried in the past many times to do just that. I found that my answers were really no answers at all. My answers could bring a temporary or partial fix to my crisis, but my strength would never bring victory. The only way to gain victory through crisis is to participate in his power.

I needed to know that my fight was not against men, but the enemy. *"For our struggle is not against flesh and blood, but against the rulers, against the authorities, against the powers of this dark world and against the spiritual forces of evil in the heavenly realms"* (Ephesians 6:12). I discovered the cause of my crisis was not men. I didn't have an earthly enemy to fight against. This battle was taking place in the heavenly realms. It was a spiritual fight. I had to learn to face the battle spiritually, not physically. This was a time when the enemy was swooping in to attempt to destroy me. It was time to fight back!

Ephesians 6:11 says, *"Put on the full armor of God so that you
can take your stand against the devil's schemes."* This was the answer I
needed. The enemy is always seeking to steal, kill, and destroy. Like
a predator, he finds those who are weak and injured and attacks with
full fury. He knew that I was weak, struggling to survive each day.
So I found his attack to be full force against me. It hurt and it was
beyond my own ability to cope with. But God, in his wisdom, had
already given me weapons to use every day. I could defend myself
against the enemy's attack and fight back. I had available to me the
full armor of God. All I needed to do was put it on and use it.

I began to put on the armor each morning. It was the first thing
I did. As I prayed, I took each piece and consciously put it on as
described in Ephesians 6. It became second nature to me. I started
with my head and worked my way down, taking each piece of the
armor and placing it around my life for that day. Each piece took on
a special meaning as I prayed.

First, I put on the helmet of salvation. Each time I did this, I realized that I was asking God to protect my mind against the onslaught
of the enemy. I needed my mind to be renewed. I asked God to help
me think about the truth of salvation and to restore the joy I had
experienced through it. I asked him to protect my thought life and
prompt me to think about him instead of the destruction I imagined.
I asked God to restore areas in my mind that had been damaged by
destructive thoughts and neglect. Each day I did this, it became easier
to abide with Christ instead of believing the lies of the enemy.

Then I put on the breastplate of righteousness. Righteousness, simply defined, means to be in right standing with God. I knew that my
own righteousness would never do that. *"All of us have become like one
who is unclean, and all our righteous acts are like filthy rags; we all shrivel
up like a leaf, and like the wind our sins sweep us away"* (Isaiah 64:6). Self-
righteousness is no righteousness at all. In order for me to be in right
standing with God, I had to appropriate the righteousness of Christ to

my life. I realized that when I put on that piece of the armor, I was literally putting on Christ's righteousness as protection. With his righteousness covering me, my heart was protected. Like King David, I prayed,
"Lord, give me an undivided heart. I want only to please you."

The next piece to put on was the belt of truth. There were many
sources of lies in my life. The enemy was lying to me by telling me
I was doomed to disaster and that I had failed God. My flesh joined
with that and lied to me saying that this situation was hopeless. I
would never recover. The world was always telling me that I didn't
measure up to its standards. There were always people more qualified
than I who fit the mold of success perfectly. There was no shortage
of lies being spoken to me. What I needed was the truth. That truth
only comes from God. I prayed each day for God to reveal his truth
to me. I wanted to know what he thought of me.

I also asked the Lord to help me speak the truth. I would tell
God that I didn't want any lies to exist in me. One day as I was praying, I said "Lord, help me to speak the truth of your Word today." It
surprised me. I really wasn't even thinking when I said that, but it
became a revelation to me. I needed to speak the truth of the Word
over my life. I began to proclaim things like, "I am a child of God.
God has plans for me. I have a future and a hope. Whom the Son
sets free is free indeed." These things are the truth. As I spoke them, I
was filled with the truth. Equally important was the fact that all evil
principalities and powers were hearing it as well. This was the truth
and it was setting me free.

The next piece of armor was one that always baffled me: "... *and
with your feet fitted with the readiness that comes from the gospel of peace*"
(Ephesians 6:15). I had always thought that when I was putting on this
part of the armor, I was putting on the shoes of the gospel. In reality, I
was putting on "*readiness* that comes from the gospel of peace." I began
to ask God to make me ready to go. He knows exactly how he has created me. He knows exactly how he has gifted me. I was asking him to

use me and the gifts that he has placed in me. Each day I needed to be ready. It is difficult to walk somewhere when you have no shoes. I needed the shoes of readiness.

I began to proclaim to God: "Here am I, send me. Here am I, use me!" This was the prayer that the prophet Isaiah declared before God as he was seeing a vision of heaven. God needed to send someone and Isaiah declared his availability. I was declaring the same thing. I was making myself available to God to be used for his purpose.

Next, I needed to take up the shield of faith: *"In addition to all this, take up the shield of faith, with which you can extinguish all the flaming arrows of the evil one"* (Ephesians 6:16). Obviously, the purpose for this piece of armor, as stated in the scripture, is to stop the "flaming arrows" of the enemy. But as I began to pray and take up this shield, I realized that I was asking God to increase my faith. I would ask the Lord to make my faith bigger. I wanted it big enough to cover my whole life and the lives of my family. I wanted faith big enough to hope and dream again.

I asked God to give me the faith of Abraham. One day I was reading in the book of Hebrews, chapter 11. There is a "Faith Hall of Fame" listed there. Abraham is a critical part of that chapter. I was reading how he obeyed God who told him to take his son Isaac away from home and sacrifice him. This was Abraham's promised son, born to him in his old age. It was a miracle that Abraham and Sarah were able to conceive a child at all in this stage of life. God had promised Abraham that from this child would come many nations and people as numerous as the stars. Yet he obeyed and took Isaac up to sacrifice him. As I was reading this, I thought, *How could Abraham obey this? He must have been thinking that God meant something else when he promised him those things. He must have thought that maybe there would be another child.* With all of these thoughts in my head, the next verse answered all those questions and suppositions: *"Abraham reasoned that God could raise the dead, and figuratively speaking, he did receive Isaac back from death"* (Hebrews 11:19). There was no situation or circumstance, no crisis, that could shake Abraham. Nothing made him waver in his faith. His faith was simple. He didn't try to figure out what God was up to. He simply obeyed and believed that if he did go through with his task to kill Isaac, God would simply bring him back to life. That was the kind of faith I wanted. This was the kind of faith I needed. This was what the shield of faith could do for me.

Finally, I would take up the sword of the Spirit. Ephesians 6:12 tells us that the sword of the spirit is the Word of God. This gave me a weapon to fight with. I could literally take back territory from the enemy with this sword. I found that the Word is applicable to every area of my life. *"For the word of God is living and active. Sharper than any double-edged sword, it penetrates even to dividing soul and spirit, joints and marrow; it judges the thoughts and attitudes of the heart"* (Hebrews 4:12).

My thoughts and attitudes are judged by the Word. If that is true, then those same thoughts and attitudes can be changed. This was the principle that sank deeply into my heart. By applying God's Word to my life, I could change. My thoughts would become his thoughts. My attitudes would change to reflect the attitudes of Jesus. The battle was taking place primarily in my mind. So when I began to apply this scripture to my thoughts, they changed. The destructive thoughts became less frequent. When they did come, they didn't affect me physically any longer. I was able to take them captive, make them obedient to Christ, and move on.

The act of daily putting on the armor of God changed my perspective of the crisis. I was able to defeat the enemy and his attack on my mind. I made a vow before the Lord during that time. I told him that I would never miss a day without putting on the armor of God. It is a vow that I have kept and will keep for the rest of my life. The value of doing this was beyond measure during my time of crisis.

A New Foundation

"See, I lay in Zion, a tested stone,
a precious cornerstone for a sure foundation;
the one who trusts will never be dismayed."
ISAIAH 28:16

When day eight came, I needed something of even more substance from God. I felt like he had given me some spiritual tools. Now I needed to know how he felt about me. What was he really working out in my life? I told the Lord that morning that I would open my Bible. Wherever it fell was where I would read. I have always laughingly referred to this as "the bmmph method." That is the act of opening up your Bible without any direction whatsoever as to where to read. I don't practice this method on a regular basis, but this seemed like an appropriate time. I was in need and I was desperate for a word from God.

My Bible fell open to Isaiah 28. I said, "Okay, Lord, here it goes." I read that chapter four times that morning. The first time through, I received very little. But as I kept reading, something happened. I experienced one of those times when the Holy Spirit made the words jump off the page and sink into my spirit. God wanted to show me some deep things about my life, and this was the right chapter to expose it.

I need to insert a little personal history here in order for you to understand what the Lord was showing me. I was raised in a Christian home. My parents both loved the Lord with all their hearts. They took all of us to church every Sunday and most Wednesday evenings. Not only did they take us to church, they lived what they believed. My mom and dad were known for their deep faith.

The church we attended while I was growing up was very solid scripturally. They taught the Word with passion. However, along with that passion came an unhealthy dose of legalism. There were many rules: We were raised to believe that we couldn't dance, go to movies, or be found in a roller skating rink. We weren't allowed to have playing cards. We didn't frequent bowling allies either. These are just a few of the rules I obeyed and believed through some very formative years.

I remember an incident that took place at school when I was in second grade. My mom was actively involved in volunteering at school. That year she was a "room mother." This meant she helped with field trips and planning activities. One of the activities offered to us was square dancing. My parents had such strong beliefs about dancing that Mom wrote a note to the school asking that I be excused from this activity because of our religious beliefs.

She handed me the note to take to school. I was to give it to my teacher. I felt conspicuous standing and watching these activities. I had faced this before with other things at school. So, conveniently, I forgot to deliver the note. I participated in the square dancing class despite my parent's disapproval. My thinking was, *what they don't know can't hurt them.* One day the dancing class was in full session in the gymnasium. To my horror, my mother walked through the gym door during the class. She saw me dancing! What was going to happen to me? Fear gripped me as I thought about the confrontation I would have with my dad.

The confrontation never came. I still do not know why. I believe my mom never told him about it. There was no consequence, but damage had been done. This event was another building block stacked on a false foundation of legalism and fear in my life. In my mind, I was doing something terrible by participating in the dance class. Being discovered filled me with fear of the consequences.

As an adult believer, I wanted to denounce religious legalism. I talked about it and taught about the snares involved. But those building blocks were stacked high on the false foundation that had been built in my life. I never thought about it. These things simply became a part of my Christian experience. Without even noticing, I was trapped behind a wall that was keeping me from a deeper relationship with Jesus. *"For it is: Do and do, do and do, rule on rule, rule on rule; a little here, a little there"* (Isaiah 28:10).

In the context of the chapter, Isaiah is telling the people that this philosophy was being taught by their corrupt priests. He goes on to say that the people had been offered a *"place of repose."* But they refused to listen.

> *So the word of the Lord to them became:*
> *Do and do, do and do,*
> *rule on rule, rule on rule;*
> *a little here, a little there—*
> *so they will go and fall backward,*
> *be injured and snared and captured."* Isaiah 28:13

The truth of this word hit me right between the eyes. I had lived my life believing this very thing! The men who taught these things in my life weren't evil. I had simply accepted these rules and allowed them to become a part of me. My actions proved that I lived by these rules more than I lived by the Spirit. I tried to do and do things to make God happy with me. I believed that my spiritual portion was *"a little here, a little there."*

That day God exposed the wall of legalism in my life. His intent was to set me free from the bondage that believing this had put me in. What a freeing experience that was! I didn't have to live by these rules any longer. I didn't have to try to please God by what I did. He is pleased with me in spite of what I do or don't do. He wants to give me more than I can even imagine. Not just a small portion.

> *So this is what the Sovereign LORD says:*
> *See I lay a stone in Zion, a tested stone,*
> *a precious cornerstone*
> *for a sure foundation,*
> *the one who trusts will never be dismayed.* Isaiah 28:16.

My old foundation was not a sure foundation. It was soft. It was a little like the man who built his house on the sand. Jesus warned the disciples about doing that. God was offering me a new foundation. It is a firm foundation. The cornerstone of this foundation is Christ himself. Jesus had always been a part of my foundation. But he wanted to be my whole foundation. He asked me if he could. I said yes.

SOME WORDS FOR YOU

The process of going through my crisis took many twists and turns. But the path of drawing near to God was clear. It wound through his Word. If I could give you one thing to count on through your time of crisis, it would be this: God's Word is stable. It is your source of strength when there is no strength to be found anywhere else. If you will allow the Holy Spirit to quicken the Word to your spirit, God will speak.

Your situation may be completely different than mine was. The issues God wants to confront in your life are probably different than mine. The one thing that remains constant in all our lives is God's Word. Each of us may *hear* God differently. He does speak uniquely to each person. I've heard people talk about hearing an audible voice. Many people have dreams. Some have visions. Others are fully aware of his *"still, small voice."* Yet all of these manifestations of God's voice must share one common theme; they must be founded on the infallible Word of God, the Bible. If you will use his Word, he will guide you through your crisis.

The spiritual battle for control of our minds is real. It takes place in all of our lives. Since the enemy has no access to your redeemed spirit, the next best course of action is to attack your mind. In order to combat this, apply God's Word. Take all those negative and destructive thoughts captive. Put on the full armor of God. Do it every day. Remember, you are putting on HIS salvation, HIS righteousness and HIS truth. HE will arm you with readiness, faith and the Word. If you will apply this to your life, God will renew your mind.

Finally, allow God to tear down unhealthy foundations in your life. What are those false foundations? What part of your life is built on sand? Mine was legalism and fear. When it was exposed, I allowed the Holy Spirit to start the demolition process. God is jealous. He does not want to share your life with any other god or thing. Allow him to expose these dark areas of your life and he will give you a new foundation with Christ himself as your Chief Cornerstone.

"For God who said, 'let light shine out of darkness,' made his light shine in our hearts to give us the light of the knowledge of the glory of God in the face of Christ" (2 Corinthians 4:6).

3
"I WILL MEET YOU"

The Great Awakening

*"The hour has come for you to wake up
from your slumber, because our salvation is
nearer now than when we first believed."*

ROMANS 13:11

Each Sunday before I attended a church service, I met with a few friends to pray. This had been my habit for several months. The purpose for meeting was to pray for the church. We would pray for the services taking place and those who were speaking and leading worship. These times became very important to me during my crisis time. These prayer times were a source of strength. I always seemed to come away having been "refreshed" by the brothers.

One Sunday morning, one of the brothers was praying that people would awaken from spiritual slumber. During the course of that prayer, he used the phrase, "the great awakening." That became the theme of our prayers that day. We prayed that God would wake up his church. We asked God to perfect us so we would truly be blameless before him.

The Lord began to speak to me about this "great awakening." The things he said to me were about my own life. During this time of crisis, God intended to wake ME up from my spiritual slumber. His desire for me was to awaken spiritual things that he had placed in me. I had allowed these gifts and calling to lie dormant. I knew they were there, but I was not moving toward his purposes for my life. I had been sidetracked by earthly things and my own desires. It was time for me to wake up to the real purpose for my life.

I could not get away from that phrase. Over and over again, it would come to mind. I was reminded of two different stories in the Bible centered on the theme of waking up.

When Jesus was nearing the time that he would be crucified, there is an account of his experience in the garden of Gethsemane. The account is found in Matthew, chapter 26. He took Peter, James, and John with him deep into the garden. Jesus was experiencing sadness and sorrow. His humanity was realizing that there was a difficult circumstance ahead. He asked the disciples to "keep watch" with him. Jesus went on to pray and cry out to the Father concerning what he was about to endure. When he came back, the disciples had fallen asleep. Jesus asked, *"Could you men not keep watch with me for one hour?"* (v. 40). He instructed them again to pray. After going and praying a second time, Jesus came back only to find the disciples sleeping again. After a third time, he rebuked them, explaining that they needed to rise and go with him.

This story spoke deeply to me. I knew God had a reason and purpose for my life. I had known early in my Christian life that God was calling me to walk with him closely. He had plans for me that I did not understand. All I had to do was walk with him and let him direct my path. Over the past several years, I had spiritually gone to sleep. I didn't lose my relationship with the Lord. I simply was not pursuing him and his purpose for my life. I had gotten distracted by my own desires and ambitions. I was being asked to wake up and walk with Christ on the road that he had prepared.

The second story involves Peter. In Acts, chapter 12, he found himself in prison. He was there for a noble cause, the cause of Christ.

I love Peter. There are many parallels between my life and calling and his. I relate to many things he went through. In this story, Peter was asleep. It seems he was unconcerned about the situation. He had full faith that God would deliver him. While he was sleeping, an angel appeared. Peter didn't notice. A light shone in the prison cell. Again, Peter did not notice. So the angel *"struck Peter on the side and woke him up"* (v. 7a). He told him to get up quickly. God was delivering him from prison. But in order for him to be set free and walk out with the angel, he needed to wake up, get up and follow God's leading.

The Lord again spoke to me through that story. I was, figuratively, in prison too. I was put there for the cause of Christ as well. I didn't know this at the time, but God had brought me to that place to launch me into a deeper relationship with him. The first thing that needed to happen was for me to awaken. I began to pray that I would wake up spiritually to the things that God wanted to create in me. If it took an angel of the Lord to whack me on the side, so be it. I was ready. This gave me new hope. I knew that the angel had awakened Peter because he was delivering him from prison. So God's desire was to deliver me from the prison of my crisis as well. In order to walk out of it, I had to wake up and go with God.

Seeking His Presence

> *"Blessed are those who have learned to acclaim you,*
> *who walk in the light of your presence, O LORD."*
> **PSALM 89:15**

In my time of crisis, God began to teach me life-changing lessons. He was drawing me into his presence. He always loved and cared for me. He did those things whether I chose to be in relationship with him or not. But it was time for me to make choices that led to him. I began to desire closeness with him. It was at that time that he brought me a new understanding of a foundational element of the Christian faith.

In some ways, I felt separated from God. The Bible told me that nothing could separate me from the love of God. I knew that, but there still seemed to be something getting in the way of the closeness I desired. Suddenly, I realized what it was—SIN. The one thing that God cannot look on is sin. When Jesus was on the cross, there came a point when he took on the sins of all mankind. It was in that moment that he cried out, *"My God, My God, why have you forsaken me?"* He was saying the same thing David did in Psalm 22:1. David found that sin separated him from the presence of the Lord. Even Jesus, God's own Son, experienced a moment when the Father could not be with him . . . because of sin.

The key to overcoming the separation from God caused by sin is repentance. I had been taught about repentance all my life. I knew the truth about it and I believed it. I found, however, that repentance had never become a part of my daily life. If I had committed some obvious sin, I would ask God to forgive me, but I never viewed those experiences as a vehicle to seeking the presence of the Lord. I had always viewed repentance as a negative but necessary act. God was about to change my understanding of what it truly meant to repent before him.

Once again, I found direction from the life of David. He was a man who understood his own need for repentance and the great reward of being in the presence of the Lord:

When I kept silent,
my bones wasted away
through my groaning all day long.
For day and night
your hand was heavy upon me;
my strength was sapped
as in the heat of summer.
Then I acknowledged my sin to you
and did not cover up my iniquity.
I said, 'I will confess

*my transgressions to the LORD'—and you forgave
the guilt of my sin.* Psalm 32:4-7.

David realized that when he attempted to hide sin from God
or even just be silent about it, there were consequences. He felt that
God's hand was heavy upon his life. However, when he confessed his
sin to God, being completely open about it, he found release. He said
that God forgave the "guilt of his sin." Something significant happened in David's life when he confessed his sin and turned away from
it. So much freedom from guilt came to him that he was able to say:
*"You are my hiding place; you will protect me from trouble and surround
me with songs of deliverance"* (Psalm 32:7).

David wrote the greatest prayer of confession and repentance ever
expressed in Psalm 51. He wrote this prayer after Nathan the prophet
came to him and exposed his sin with Bathsheba. This was one of the
lowest points in David's life. He had sinned against God and he knew
it. He had tried to hide it even to the point of having Bathsheba's husband, Uriah, killed. But he knew that he was separated from God as a
result of his sin, and he wanted to seek the presence of the Lord again.

The Lord showed me through this psalm of David how liberating the act of repentance is. I learned that it is not a negative thing
or a chore to be dreaded. It is an act that literally draws me closer to
God and his presence. It removes any barriers between us. I saw three
simple aspects to David's prayer. I began to pray these every day. I still
make these three things a part of my daily prayers of repentance. I have
found the act of praying these things draws me closer to the Lord.

1. HAVE MERCY ON ME (I'M CRYING OUT)
*"Have mercy on me O God, according to your
unfailing love; according to your great compassion
blot out my transgressions."*
PSALM 51:1

I began to ask God to forgive my sins. I asked him to have mercy on me. In other words, "God, don't give me what I deserve." This is what mercy really is. It was important for me to understand that I was not coming to a God who is a prison keeper. He was not about to slam the prison door behind me and forget me forever. I was not begging for my life at the hands of an executioner. I was coming to a God who loves me beyond anything I can even imagine. His love for me is absolutely unfailing. I will never be separated from his love. He is compassionate. In other words, he WANTS to forgive my sin. The only sin that has not been forgiven is the sin that I have not confessed before him.

His mercy is everlasting. It is always available. He wants to pour out his mercy on me every day. As I began to appropriate this prayer each day, I was released from past sin. I didn't have to keep asking him to forgive the same old sins. It had already been done. I was simply asking him to forgive my sins from that day. All others had already been covered by his great mercy through the precious blood of Jesus. All the separation that sin causes was stripped away and I began to live in that close relationship that I had always desired.

2. Cleanse Me (I'm Soaking In)

"Cleanse me with hyssop, and I will be clean;
wash me, and I will be whiter than snow."
Psalm 51:7

Starting in first grade, I attended Vacation Bible School every summer. It always took place the first week following our dismissal from school for the summer. I grew up in a small town and there was only one Bible school offered. It was at the local Baptist church. I can still remember the sight of many children gathered in the basement of the church doing various activities and being taught the truths of the Bible. I remember the smell of paste and finger paint. And I still remember the sound of the music as we played triangles, recorders and tambourines. But most of all, I remember the flannel board.

We would all gather for the lesson as the teacher would tell us about Jesus and all the things he did and said. One particular lesson was taught over and over again. The teacher would illustrate the state of our lives as sinners by putting a black heart made of felt on the flannel board. Then she would explain that Jesus had come to take away our sins by bleeding and dying on the cross. She illustrated this by placing a red heart over the black one. Finally, she would say that because of what Jesus had done for us, we no longer had to live with black and sinful hearts, we were washed in his blood, and he had given us clean, pure hearts. Over the black heart and the red one would be placed a bright white heart.

David's prayer is a cry to God to do in his life just what my Bible school teacher had illustrated. He knew that since God had already shown mercy to him and blotted out his sins, there was a cleansing available. The word used here for "wash" literally means 'to baptize'. David was asking God to cleanse him as a result of already having his sins removed.

As I began to use this scripture in prayer, I found myself simply being quiet before the Lord and receiving his forgiveness. I confessed my sins and asked for mercy. Now I was asking for his cleansing and immersing myself in his forgiveness. What a wonderful feeling! I experienced the cleansing from sin in a new and fresh way each day.

New boldness came as I began to proclaim that I had been cleansed. I joyfully raised my voice to declare that I had been washed in the blood of Jesus. This is something that David could not say. He could only foreshadow the blessing and grace I would receive because of the blood of Jesus shed for me. *"If we confess our sins, he is faithful and just to forgive our sins and cleanse us from all unrighteousness"* (1 John 1:9).

3. CREATE IN ME (I'M GIVING UP)
*"Create in me a pure heart, O God,
and renew a steadfast spirit within me."*
PSALM 51:10

In this verse is found one of the greatest attributes of God. He is
not in the repair business. When I come to him confessing my sin and
asking for his cleansing, he is going to make me brand new. His intent
is to create something new in me every day. I love this truth about
God. He has been, is, and will always be a creator. He didn't stop
creating after he made the earth, the universe, the animals, and Adam
and Eve. He is still creating something new in me as I yield my spirit,
soul, and flesh to him. In the New Testament, we read, *"Therefore,
if anyone is in Christ, he is a new creation; the old has gone, the new has
come"* (2 Corinthians 5:17).

I began to ask God to create new things in me. I asked him to give
me an upright spirit. I asked for a meek and humble spirit. I desired
more gifts, talents, and creativity to be birthed in my life. Each day as
I prayed, I sensed the Lord creating a new life for me. I didn't have to
yield to the flesh and live the way I always had. I didn't have to react
in anger. Fear did not have to be a part of my life any longer. Those
things and more were being replaced by the new creations that he was
building in me. All I really needed to do was give up. All the strength
I thought I had in me had to go. I was throwing myself on the mercy
of Almighty God, asking him to cleanse me and allowing him to create a new life for me.

SOME WORDS FOR YOU
In times of crisis, it is vitally important that you seek the presence
of the Lord. As Christians, we need not try to find his presence. It is
always with us in the person of the Holy Spirit. Let me assure you,
God has not left you. When you made your commitment to Christ,

he deposited the Holy Spirit in you. Even if you feel separated from God, you need to understand that he is right there waiting for you to meet with him.

Seeking God's presence is not difficult. It is simply removing anything that separates us from him. As I explained earlier, those things are sin. I am on a mission to proclaim to Christians everywhere that repentance is not a negative thing. It is not an act reserved for special days or big events. Repentance should be a regular part of our daily lives. There is no shame involved with repentance. God has created for us a way to remove any obstacles (sins) that come between us and his presence. He has freely offered us the forgiveness of sin. All we have to do is confess our sins to him, allow him to cleanse us, and ask him to create new lives for us. Make confession and repentance a part of your daily prayers.

Have you ever had the opportunity to spend time in a hot tub? After a long day at work or with your daily duties, it can be the most relaxing experience available. As you recline there, you soak in the warm relaxing jets of water. After spending some time there, you are refreshed and all the aches and pains disappear.

Seeking God's presence through the act of repentance is like sitting in the hot tub. Once you have cried out for God's mercy and confessed your sin, you can rest and soak in his forgiveness. It is an incredible experience to allow God to cleanse and wash your sins away! You see, repentance is not a one-sided event. God is actively involved in the process. He is pouring out his mercy, love and compassion. He is washing and cleansing you. He is creating new things in you to replace the void left by sin. When you repent, just relax and soak in the presence of the Lord.

David said; *"You forgave the GUILT of my sin."* Please understand that God does not hold confessed sin against us. He keeps no records. Any guilt you may feel from sin that he has already forgiven is not from God. It is simply a plan by the enemy of our souls to keep you bound in a spiritual prison. Brothers and sisters, allow God to forgive the guilt of your sin as well as the sin itself. There is no longer ANY condemnation. Do not allow the enemy to propagate his lies within you!

You may feel that your circumstance is a prison. You may feel trapped. In fact, you may not see any way out of the situation. But know this; God has already prepared a way out of the prison of your crisis. He is opening the doors to allow you to walk with him through and ultimately out of your circumstance. Although you may not yet see it, there is victory awaiting you.

It is time to be awakened. If you have gone through a time of feeling separated from God, please seek him again. Like Peter, you have to wake up in order to follow God out of your circumstance. He is coming for you and he has already cleared the path for your deliverance. Look to him and follow him as he leads you out of captivity and into the victory that he has prepared for you.

You may not feel that you have been called by God. You may feel like you are destined to live a *normal* Christian life, nothing special, just living for him the best you can. But God has placed a unique call in each person. You fill a spot in his church that no one else can fill. We are the body of Christ. Each one of us has a place. He has called each of us to be ministers. Allow him to create in you the gifts, talents and abilities that he wants you to have to complete his purpose for your life.

There is a purpose for crisis. God does not want us to just escape the prison. He wants us to be led through the crisis, out of the captivity we feel, and into a brand new freedom. If you will begin to view your situation this way, you will find that there is tremendous hope. You can be refreshed and equipped through difficult circumstances to fulfill God's unique call for your life.

4

'"I HAVE NEW DREAMS FOR YOU"

What Are My Dreams?

"And afterward, I will pour out my Spirit on all people.
Your sons and daughters will prophecy, your old men will
dream dreams, your young men will see visions."

JOEL 2:28

What are my dreams? I don't mean the kind I have every night, only to wake up in the morning and forget all of them. I mean dreams for my life, the kind of things that are thought about often. They are the ones that speak of the future and motivate me to get up every day and pursue them. I couldn't think of any. It had been so long since I had even thought about such things that they were just distant memories. I needed to rediscover the power of dreaming. *"Where there is no vision, the people perish"* (Proverbs 29:18 KJV).

As I began to pray about dreams, the phrase, "hopes and dreams" came to mind. The more I thought about it, the more I realized that they really are one and the same. You cannot have dreams unless you hope, and you cannot have hope unless there are dreams to hope for. So I asked the Lord to remind me again of my dreams. I wanted to have a fresh sense of what those dreams were for my life. The above scripture is one that I have heard my entire life. It had been quoted many times in sermons and in conversation with others. I believed it, but I never really understood the impact of that statement. Finally, it occurred to me; this is really about revelation. It has to do with vision, dreams, and revelation that had been planted in me by God himself. These were not selfish things. They were inspired in me by the Holy Spirit. It was in these dreams that I also found hope that God indeed was going to deliver me from my crisis.

When I really searched my heart to rediscover these dreams, I found that the things God had put in me were all about ministry. I had been called by God, at the age of eighteen to "[equip] *the saints to do the work of ministry*" (Ephesians 4:11 NKJV). I had never lost that calling. Whenever I tried to get away from it, God would remind me again that I still had a purpose in his kingdom. But that call had taken a back seat to other things in my life. Now it was time to believe the dream again.

At first, it didn't seem like the kind of dream I was thinking of. I expected to remember some things about places I might travel or important people I might meet. But none of that came. When I thought about it, fulfilling my call to ministry was the only thing that had ever really been a dream in my heart. I came to realize that at the age of fifty-one, I was finally seeing the destiny that God had for me. I realized this dream was an eternal one. The dream would not die with me when I leave here and go to be with the Lord. It would carry on in the lives of people who are touched by a life that would truly be "living the dream."

Don't Look Back

> *"But Lot's wife looked back, and she became a pillar of salt."*
> **Genesis 19:26**

I knew the story of Sodom and Gomorrah well. From my days in Sunday school, we were taught this lesson from the Bible. The account in Genesis 18-19 tells us that Abraham pleaded with God not to destroy the cities. After a period of negotiation, God told Abraham that if there were but ten righteous men in the cities, he would not destroy them. So God sent two angels to visit Sodom. Lot, the nephew of Abraham, met them at the city gate. The cities were so corrupt with immorality that Lot would not allow the angels to stay outside in the town square. They were taken to his house for the night. Corrupt men from the city came to Lot's house and told him to send out the two "men" so they could have sex with them. Lot refused, and after an ugly confrontation, the angels struck the men blind. They led Lot and his family out of the city safely and told them to flee to the mountains. God rained down fire from heaven and destroyed those cities.

The angels told Lot and his family specifically to not look back toward the cities while God was destroying them. But Lot's wife did look back and immediately was turned into a pillar of salt. As a result of her disobedience to the commands of the Lord, she died.

You may be familiar with this story. You may also be asking, "What does this story have to do with a time of crisis?" I asked that same question the day this story came to me. It flooded my mind and I could not stop thinking about it. So I asked the Lord to reveal to me just what he was saying. Again, he was faithful to show me exactly why this story had been brought to my attention.

In my crisis time, I found myself looking back to the past. What could I have done differently to avoid the crisis? What did I do wrong? Why is God punishing me? I asked these questions of myself continually. As a result of that, I was simply reliving the past and living in a place of defeat. I would never enter into the new dreams the Lord had for me if I continued to look back.

The answers to these questions may never be known. But one answer was certain. God was not punishing me. He seized the opportunity of a circumstance to bring me to a place where I would be completely alone with him. All of the distractions were gone. I had nothing else but him to depend on. And that was exactly where he needed me to be. In order to restore my dreams, he needed to get me to a place where all my attention was focused on him.

The apostle Paul taught this truth: *"Forgetting what is behind and straining toward what is ahead, I press on toward the goal to win the prize for which God has called me heavenward in Christ Jesus"* (Philippians 3:13b-14). I realized that God was calling me to understand this and change the way I was thinking. He wanted me to press on, not be weighed down by perceived past failures. Whatever sin I had committed was already forgiven and forgotten. He was challenging me to join him in forgetting my past failures and moving into his plan for my future.

The Lord was careful to tell me that he had NEW dreams for me. He wanted me to enter into something that was completely birthed in his will for my life. How could I enter into that place if I continued to relive the past? It was at this point I clearly heard the Lord speak to me in his gentle and quiet way, *"Barry, when you relive the past, it only brings death to your spirit."* At that moment, I made a conscious decision to stop reliving the past and the circumstances that brought me to this place. From that point on, I was going to live for the future. It gave me new hope. Remember, hopes and dreams go together. When I finally gave the past to God, he began to open up the future to me. My hopes and dreams returned.

My past was not a horrible experience. I had been a Christian for many years. I had a wonderful wife and family. We had many great experiences together. I had gone where the Lord led and my life had been good. The job that had just ended had been a great blessing to us. It was a good experience and a financial boost. So the problem was not the past. The problem was—I continued to relive the past. When I did that, I wasn't thinking of the good things, I was reliving the bad ones. To be released from that trap put me in a new position. The past was simply the past. There were good things and bad things, but it all contributed to my growth. Each day I reminded myself, "Don't look back!"

A RESTORATION PROJECT

> *"Do not conform any longer to the pattern of this world,*
> *but be transformed by the renewing of your mind.*
> *Then you will be able to test and approve what*
> *God's will is—his good, pleasing and perfect will."*
>
> ROMANS 12:2

I like to walk. You may notice that many of the things the Lord speaks to me come while I am out walking. I don't know, maybe it is a tranquil time, a few moments when nothing else is really that important. But when I am walking, I can get in touch with God. It seems he is right there walking beside me, having a conversation with me as if I were talking with a friend. Some of the most important spiritual events in my life were initiated while I was walking and talking to God.

It was one of those walks that began a vital process in my life. I was praying, reminding God of the situation I was in. It's funny how that helps. Now God knew full well the situation I was in. He was already working in my life dramatically, using this crisis to change me. But somehow, it just helped to explain it to him again. Suddenly, I became aware of some truths about my life during this crisis. It was as if the Holy Spirit pointed out three very important things to me. As I began to ponder these things, they became the elements of a restoration project in my life.

1. I HAD ENCUMBRANCES.

This particular word is not one that I regularly use. I wasn't quite sure of the meaning. But a picture soon came to me that illustrated it perfectly. I saw myself with shackles attached to my wrists and ankles. The shackles were attached to chains and on the ends of the chains were heavy balls made of steel. These balls were not so heavy that they would keep me from moving at all. But they were heavy enough to make it difficult to walk and move freely. The Lord was showing me what being *encumbered* meant.

In my Christian life, I had always tried to live the best I could. But along the way, I had picked up some things that became encumbrances to me. Most of these things had to do with other people. In various ways, through relationships, I had taken on things that inhibited my walk with God. Some of these things included financial agreements I had entered into with people that ended badly. Others were relationships with people I had been very close to. Through circumstances, these relationships ended up being strained or even broken.

I needed to break the chains of these encumbrances. The first step to breaking them was to repent. If I had done anything in these broken relationships that dishonored God, I needed to have his forgiveness. So I began to recount these things before the Lord. His forgiveness, of course, was instant and glorious. The restoration of relationships is a tenuous and fragile thing. I discovered that moving with direction from God was paramount. Although I was dealing with the pain and destruction of certain relationships, the other people were in different spiritual places than I. So I became content to allow God to lead me in the restoration and renewing of old relationships.

2. MY MIND WAS MY OWN WORST ENEMY.

I have already described the destructive thoughts I dealt with during this crisis. But there was much more than just those thoughts that were hindering me. Ephesians 4:23 says, *"Be made new in the attitude of your minds."* I realized that I was still living by old attitudes. The old way of thinking and bad attitudes had to be dealt with. The only way this was going to happen was through a renewing process. The author of that process is the Holy Spirit. He could help me destroy those destructive thoughts and change old attitudes.

I began to be aware of attitudes that I had lived with my whole life. I had always been quick to get angry. It didn't last very long, but I would react to situations or comments in an unhealthy way. Of course, these events often involved my wife, Cathy. The Lord began to show me that many of the ways I reacted in my relationship with her were wrong. These were habits I had developed in my life and then just chose to accept as "the way I am." The reality was that those were wrong attitudes and God had something much better for me.

I discovered that I also had vengeful thoughts. The termination of my employment was a very ugly experience. It left me feeling worthless and dishonored. I reacted to that by having thoughts of taking vengeful actions against people. Of course, I knew I would never do such things. But it became, in a sordid way, fun to think such things. How could a man who loves God have such evil thoughts? They were a product of a mind that was still thinking the way the world thinks. In fact, I was even thinking the way the enemy wanted me to think. This was destructive to me. It was an evil, worldly attitude that needed to be changed. Again, the source of strength and change was the Holy Spirit.

Now, you may be thinking, "This guy really had big issues!" Well, yes I did . . . and still do. But I am being perfectly honest about the process that I went through. All of us need to have our minds renewed. If we are really honest with ourselves, we will all find areas of our minds that are evil. It is these areas that the Lord wants to renew. He wants to change us so we begin to think more like he does. The process involves discovering those areas, recognizing the need, and allowing the Holy Spirit to renew us.

3. GOD WANTED ME TO BE COMPLETELY DEPENDENT ON HIM.

From the day I lost my job, I knew that God was asking me to depend on him. There had been times in my life when I thought I was completely trusting him. But when it came to crunch time, I would always act in my own strength and find a way out of my situation that seemed to work. But this time the admonition from God was clear. *"Depend on me,"* he said. On this day, he reaffirmed that direction for me.

When I dealt with difficult circumstances before, the way out always seemed to involve myself or someone else. The problem with this course was the fix was always temporary. It never seemed to solve anything; it simply prolonged the inevitable. If I were in need of a job, I would go out and find temporary work or seek the help of friends. I am not saying that either one of these things is wrong. But in this time of my life, God was clearly asking me to not attempt to rectify the situation on my own. He wanted me to trust him completely and not receive anything less. His solution to my crisis was the perfect one. Anything I could do in my own strength would be less than what his desire was for me.

Once again, David's writing in Psalm 27 comforted me and solidified this direction: *"Wait for the Lord; be strong and take heart and wait for the Lord"* (Psalm 27:14). No matter what my flesh was telling me, the only option I had was to wait for the Lord. This verse gave me confidence that indeed he was coming for me. He had not forgotten me. He had not deserted me. There was coming a moment when he would show up and completely deliver me from my circumstance.

When I was four years old, our family went on a vacation together. My dad's idea of a vacation was a road trip. We would drive four hundred miles, find a hotel and get up the next morning to drive another four hundred miles. Although grueling, these vacations are still some of my treasured memories.

One day, we had stopped at the hotel for the night. It was a hot day in Nevada, and of course we had no air conditioning in the car. So the family went to the swimming pool at the hotel to cool off. I did not know how to swim, so I sat on the edge of the pool with my feet dangling in the water. I remember saying to my dad, "Daddy,

I want to jump in the water." Now my dad knew that I had no idea how to swim. But he answered, "Okay, go ahead." So after getting permission, I thought it must be a good idea. I jumped into the deep end of the pool and of course immediately sank to the bottom. I can still remember the series of events. It seemed like I was under the water for an eternity. But really, it was only a few seconds. When I reached the bottom of the pool, I pushed off the concrete with my legs to propel me toward the top. My dad was there, reaching for me before I even reached the surface. He pulled me out of the water with his strong arm.

This story illustrates exactly what was happening in my crisis. Although it seemed like I was drowning in the circumstance, my Father was right there all along, with his strong arm, waiting to pull me out of the deep waters. He would rescue me. My own strength was not enough. Just as I had depended on my dad to pull me out of the water, I had to depend on God to rescue me from the waters of my crisis. He would not leave me. He would rescue me at just the right time. I had to wait for him.

This chapter began with my discovery of new dreams. God wanted to encourage me to dream again. In order for that to happen, I had to stop reliving the past and allow him to have those areas of my life that needed to be healed. My dreams and my future lay completely in his hands. The freedom to dream returned. It became a turning point in my life. God was reminding me that he had new ones for me. If I were willing, he would give me new hope and big dreams.

Some Words for You

What are your dreams? I have shared here that my dreams were all centered in ministry. That certainly does not set me apart from you or anyone else. All of us have dreams. My encouragement for you is to begin to think of these dreams as ideas from God. I believe that God wants to use every one of us who are Christians to fulfill his work on the earth. Will you begin to view your dreams as pathways to accomplish this mission?

As an example, you may have a great desire to travel through Europe. Maybe you want to see every country on that continent. There is certainly nothing wrong with that. In fact, having gone through a time of crisis in your life, this dream may have resurfaced. Can you see this dream as potential to touch the world for the cause of Christ? I do. God wants to give you the desire of your heart. If we will allow his will to permeate our dreams, we will find that what we want in life is exactly what God wants us to have.

If you have stopped dreaming as a result of your crisis or simply because you are feeling there is no hope, I encourage you to start dreaming again. Ask God to help you. Ask him to refresh those dreams in your life. Ask him to give you new ones. These dreams are all wrapped up in the hope we have in Jesus. Rediscover your dreams.

I have talked to many people who have a long list of failures in their lives. Some of them are financial struggles; others are broken marriages or relationships. Still others have come from backgrounds of drug addiction and criminal acts. But I can honestly say this: It will become death to you if you continue to look back and live in the past. God wants to use your failures to create what he intended for you. He wants us to live in victory. Begin to view your past, even your crisis, as ingredients in God's master plan to perfect and use your life for his glory.

In reality, all of us are restoration projects. Many of us have spent many years destroying what and who God created us to be. God is in the business of restoring you. He wants you to be the person he created you to be. We are all working out our salvation. God's grace has covered us. Now let's allow the Holy Spirit to change us into the people God predestined us to be.

5
"I AM BUILDING YOUR FAITH"

The Seeds of Faith
"Now faith is the substance of things hoped for,
the evidence of things not seen."
HEBREWS 11:1 NKJV

What exactly is faith? Of course, we know that it is the foundation of our Christian experience. But how does it actually work? What could I do to increase the faith I had? These were all questions I wanted to receive answers for. God had brought me through many learning experiences during my crisis. Now he desired to give me new faith to receive the things he had already accomplished in me, and to expect more.

The problem I faced, however, was the overwhelming feeling that I had little faith. The crushing defeat I had endured was fresh in my mind and heart. Any faith I thought I had was buried under the rubble created by the circumstance. But God had already shown me the reality that I must return to the beginning. I had to give up everything I thought I knew and submit to his work in me. I needed to be honest with him. I simply told him that I had little faith left. I was hurting and left devastated by a crushing blow to my identity.

The process of removing all things that were not centered on Jesus had already begun. I was forced to look at many things I had built my

Christian existence on and determine if I had received those things from God or created them as a convenient crutch. Faith was one of those things. My concept of faith in God was founded on things I had learned. These things had value, but they were not my own. My faith was shaken to the core and I needed a deep faith of my own. That is exactly where God needed me to be so he could build a sure foundation of faith within me.

The process I was going through was painful yet rich with the blessings of the Lord. And although there were things that needed to be torn down in my life, there were things he wanted to build in me as well. Faith is a building block. I know that when I gave my life to Christ when I was seventeen, I exercised faith in God for the first time. I put my full trust in him, gave up my pride and reluctance, and believed him. I believed his word to me: *"For it is by grace you have been saved, through faith—and this not from yourselves, it is the gift of God"* (Ephesians 2:8). I experienced the seed of faith that the Holy Spirit had placed in me for that moment.

As I moved on in my Christian life, some faith was added. I began to believe God's Word. I knew that he spoke to me and that I could depend on it. But in order to live through this time of crisis and get beyond it, I needed more faith than I had ever had—a new abiding kind.

As I look back on this time in my life, I am very thankful to the Lord for the things he taught me in regard to faith. The lessons and words he imparted changed the course of the rest of my life. God intended to teach me life-changing principles. He was using a crisis to bring me to a point where I recognized my great need for him. I needed to experience change in my Christian life. God was about to rebuild my foundation of faith.

ABRAHAM'S FAITH

By faith Abraham, when God tested him, offered Isaac as a sacrifice. He who had received the promises was

about to sacrifice his one and only son, even though God had
said to him, "It is through Isaac that your offspring
will be reckoned." Abraham reasoned that God
could raise the dead, and figuratively speaking,
he did receive Isaac back from death.

HEBREWS 11:17-19

I wanted big faith. I wanted enough faith that I could live through my crisis time and not only stand firm, but actually grow in faith. I needed more faith than I had ever used before. I needed faith the size of Abraham's. But what was it? What was different about his faith that put him in the "Hall of Fame" of all the Bible characters? When we think of examples of faith, we always remember Abraham. The thing that highlighted his life was his incredible faith.

Think about the kind of faith Abraham had. God told him that he would be the father of many nations. At that time, he was well along in years and Sarah, his wife, was well past her childbearing years. There were some failures. Sarah struggled with the idea and gave her servant, Hagar, to Abraham. Their thought was that surely this would be a way that the promise could be fulfilled. However, this was not God's plan. He had a perfect one. Even through this, Abraham still believed God. Sarah did become pregnant and Abraham's promise was fulfilled in the person of his promised son, Isaac. But now did God really want him to sacrifice his only son? Abraham could have said no. He could have kept Isaac at a safe distance and not obeyed God. But he chose to believe God through faith. His faith in the matter became complete when he took Isaac away to the place appointed for the sacrifice. As we know, God spared Abraham the grief of taking his son. And Abraham proved his faith through what he did.

James the apostle tells us, about Abraham, *"Do you see that faith was working together with his works, and by works faith was made complete"*

(James 2:22 NKJV). Abraham is the epitome of faith. He not only believed God, he responded by obeying what he knew God was saying. I love the insight of the writer of Hebrews. He knew that Abraham had so much faith in God that even if he sacrificed his only son, God could and would raise him from the dead. Nothing stopped Abraham's faith. Nothing caused him to question the voice of God. He simply knew what God had promised him and he obeyed.

I understood the faith of Abraham and began praying that I would have that kind of faith, but I had a problem. I was not confident enough in my ability to really hear God's voice of direction to me. I was in the middle of a crisis and all of my energy was being devoted to just surviving each day. I wanted to have faith like Abraham, but it seemed out of reach. God was clearly encouraging me every day. He was there supporting me, but receiving direction was another matter. It just didn't seem like I was receiving those words that would clearly show me where to go and what to do. I needed income, but no direction came. I needed a job, but none became available. What kind of faith was God trying to teach me? I surely couldn't expect to have the faith of Abraham in my condition.

THE FAITH OF RAHAB

"Likewise, was not Rahab the harlot also justified by works when she received the messengers and sent them out another way?"

JAMES 2:25

Rahab? Who is Rahab? I knew the story, but it never occurred to me that she would be used as an example of faith, even to be mentioned with Abraham. I decided to explore her story.

Rahab lived in Jericho at the time when the children of Israel were about to cross the Jordan River, concluding their forty-year desert wanderings. She made her living as a prostitute and was, doubtless, despised by many in the city. She took notice of the events. People in Jericho knew that the Israelites were there. There was talk about them and the God of Israel. That talk included the idea that the God of Israel had given their city to the Israelites and Jericho would surely be defeated.

Meanwhile, two spies were dispatched by the Israelites to enter the land and report back what they had found. They entered Jericho and soon found themselves being sought after by the locals. Their lives were in danger. They searched for a place of refuge and found it in the house of Rahab the harlot. She offered her help in return for a guarantee that her family would be spared the coming disaster. As she spoke with the spies, she noted that everyone in the city was saying that the God of Israel was going to defeat Jericho at the hands of his people. She told them this was her reason for the willingness to give them shelter and send them off in another direction to escape the wrath of the locals.

Rahab was included in the lineage of Jesus himself. This act of hers was later to be remembered as an act of faith. I had never thought of it that way before. She was not one of the children of Israel. The God of Israel was new to her. Yet she did something that qualified as faith and was credited to her as righteousness. What was this all about and how could it apply to me?

As I began to think about this story, I understood that there was another aspect of faith. Rahab had evidence. The evidence was there that her city was going to be overthrown by these people who served a big God. In response to this evidence, she acted by hiding the spies and helping them escape. Now this was a kind of faith that I could experience myself. It didn't take a clear word from God to use this kind of faith. It took evidence. If I could see the evidence of something God was doing and if I acted on what I saw, that would be faith. This was a new kind of freedom. I had always been waiting to get that clear direction from God before I acted. That often prevented me from moving because I was unsure. But this new kind of faith released me to enter into a new blessing.

An opportunity to experience new faith presented itself in just a few short days. I received a phone call from my daughter. She was frantic as she shared with me that her baby boy of eight months was throwing up and lethargic with a very high fever. I advised her to take him immediately to the emergency room at a local hospital. She needed me to help because her husband was not yet home. So I got in my car and drove across town to her house. When I arrived, she was already putting my little grandson into the car to head to the hospital. When I saw him, I was shocked. He was so lethargic that he could not stay awake. I called his name and got no response. I cradled his face in my hands to see if he would respond. No change. As I touched him, I realized that he was incredibly hot from fever. Right there, in the back seat of the car, I laid my hands on him and prayed. I cried out to the Lord, through tears, asking him to please heal my grandson. After praying, my son-in-law arrived and they left for the hospital.

Two hours later, I received another phone call from her. She was at the hospital and Dylan, my grandson, had just been examined by the doctors. She explained that as she drove toward the hospital, he began to be more responsive and alert. By the time she arrived, he felt cool to the touch. When the doctors examined him, they found no fever. He was responsive and alert. He drank juice and appeared to be acting normally.

I was thrilled. I began to thank God for healing Dylan. I checked with my daughter the next day. He was fine and never exhibited these symptoms again. God had healed him.

There was a time earlier in my life when I had this same kind of simple faith. I was in my twenties and Cathy and I had three small children. The youngest daughter was just five months old. She could not crawl, but rolled over and could kind of get herself into crawling position. One day the children were all playing together. The older two began to push my younger daughter over to assist her in her rolling efforts. Suddenly, we heard her scream. She had gotten her arm caught underneath herself and her shoulder had dislocated.

I swept her up in my arms, carried her to a table to change her diaper and prepared to take her to the hospital. I remember crying out to God. It wasn't an eloquent prayer at all. It was simply, "Jesus, please heal Kristen!" I turned around to get a fresh diaper and when I looked at her again, she had stopped crying, had rolled over and was pushing herself up into crawling position right there on the changing table! God had heard my cries and healed her instantly.

Those were days when I had a simple faith. It wasn't complicated or confused with over-thought doctrine. I simply believed God could do it and in desperation cried out to him. He responded and something miraculous took place. What happened to that simple, effective kind of faith? Somewhere along the line, it got complicated and fruitless.

Through the experience with my grandson, I learned that I had a new, growing faith in my life. God used his sickness to remind me of a time when I had that personal, simple faith. Then, instead of being caught in the trap of only believing God and never acting, I saw the evidence in front of me; my grandson was sick and God is the Great Healer. I knew how to pray and that prayer, offered in faith, released the healing power of God into Dylan's life. You see, my prayer of faith worked together with my belief that God could heal. When I saw the evidence that healing was needed, I acted, and my faith was made complete.

Since that time, I have learned a great deal about myself, my growing faith, and how to appropriate the power of the Holy Spirit through acting in faith. I now know that it is okay to act on my belief in God when I see evidence that that elicits a faith response from me. Since that experience, I have acted on my faith many times. I have seen clear evidence and I have begun to respond by exercising my faith. God was laying a foundation in my life that would change me forever. Faith is a growing and vital part of me. I learn something new each day about faith and how to actively use it in my life. This newfound faith would propel me through my time of crisis.

Some Words for You

Allow God to lay foundations in your life during your time of crisis. When you are in the midst of crisis, many things are happening. You find yourself consumed with the issues of the circumstance. It can be a continual weight on your shoulders. But if you will allow God to build you in areas of your life while you are in the midst of the crisis, you will be setting the stage for a growing relationship with Jesus and victory through your circumstance.

This chapter has been my attempt to share with you the amazing growth of faith in my life. That growth took place in the middle of my crisis. Some things were being torn down in my life but God was building faith in me at the same time. This same experience can be yours even in the depths of your crisis. If you will ask him for more faith, he will give it to you. I believe we need a new understanding of faith. If you are at all like I was, you may be afraid to act on the evidence you see because you are unsure God is asking you to do so. I tell you—be free from that. God, the Creator of the universe, the Maker of everything and the Redeemer of our souls is much bigger than your fears.

Faith is built by acting. There may be a process that includes some failure. But that is okay. If you act on something you believe and you see the evidence that faith is required, go for it. If you are wrong, it becomes a growing experience. But don't let that deter you from acting on your faith. The only way you will truly grow in the area of faith is by practicing it. Think of it this way: When you first gave your heart to Jesus, two things happened. First, you believed in your heart that Jesus was real and that you needed him. Then you told someone about it. Romans 10:9-10 tells us that this is the initial process of beginning a relationship with God. Notice that first you believe and then you act on that belief by confessing with your mouth. That is simple faith and the process never changes. You will continue to use that pattern for the rest of your life.

Please allow me to give you a couple of basic math equations about faith. These are things I learned during my crisis time. I have shared them with you already. Now let's make it simple.

Hearing God's voice + Obeying = Faith. This is the faith of Abraham.

Evidence + Action = Faith. This is the faith that Rahab had.

Belief in God + Faith = Righteousness. *"Abraham believed God, and it was accounted to him for righteousness"* (James 2:23).

When you begin to use your faith, good things happen. God shows up. He honors your obedience to believe him and act on that belief. When you and I learn this, it is credited to us as righteousness. Allow your faith to grow and every part of your life will increase as well.

6
"I HAVE PLANS FOR YOU"

Overcoming the Desire to Panic

"For I know the plans I have for you," declares the LORD,"
plans to prosper you and not to harm you,
plans to give you hope and a future."

JEREMIAH 29:11

In any crisis situation, the one thing that will bring the worst possible outcome is panic. In severe disasters, many people lose their lives, not from the event itself, but from the panic that ensues afterward. I have seen reports of fires that erupted in public buildings, collapses of sports stadium seating and other kinds of disasters. Many of the lives that are lost happen as a result of the panic. People are trampled by others or make poor decisions that cost them their lives.

Panic is dangerous. Although I had not experienced anything as dramatic as an earthquake, fire or tsunami, I still dealt with an overwhelming desire to allow panic to take over. I had lost something that contributed to my self-worth. I had lost my ability to provide for my wife and family. Each day lacked a sense of purpose. I was not getting up, getting ready, and going to work. As the breadwinner in my family, that left a tremendous void. After only a few weeks, I found myself beginning to panic.

The reason I felt the urge to panic was based in the fact that I did not know what the future held for us. The outcome of my crisis was uncertain. I asked myself questions that I could not answer. Would we survive financially? Would we lose everything? Would we be forced to move away from our home and family? I did not have the answers to these questions. This added to my ever-growing fear of the situation.

Although I didn't have the answers to my question, I knew someone who did. As I was reading my Bible one day, I came across Jeremiah 29:11. I knew that particular verse well, but had not thought of it as direction or help for me. As I read it that day, something happened that took away the urge to panic. I became aware of the fact that my path was already set in the sight of God. He already knew what would happen to me and where he would lead me.

There was a comfort in knowing that God already had a pathway for me. It occurred to me that the opposite of panic is comfort and peace. Psalm 57:1 says, *"Have mercy on me, O God, have mercy on me, for in you my soul takes refuge. I will take refuge in the shadow of your wings until the disaster has passed."* I found that place of comfort, contentment and peace in God. I spent time with him every day. He knew my fragile state. Sometimes, I read my Bible, other times, I prayed, and still other times, I simply sat quietly with the Lord. Not every time was productive. I have to confess that there were times I came away feeling worse than when I started. This usually happened when I began to focus on the severity of the circumstance instead of being with my Father. I discovered, however, what it really meant to take refuge in the shadow of his wings.

I found great comfort in two things I knew about God. One I mentioned already. God loves me. In fact, he broods over me just as a mother bird would brood over her eggs and young chicks. This is the word picture painted by the writers of the Psalms. I can always depend on the fact that God loves and cares for me. There is a real place of security in that. Psalm 32:7 says, *"You are my hiding place; you will protect me from trouble and surround me with songs of deliverance."*

In the midst of my trial, I needed a hiding place. It is a place of shelter in the arms of the Savior. That hiding place can be found nowhere else. I learned that every other place I attempted to find that security was not a hiding place, but rather a place of escape. I could not escape my crisis, but I found somewhere to hide from the storm. That place was in the arms of my Father. I also discovered that God is absolute truth. He does not lie. He does not tell partial truths. He does not mislead me. Instead, *"The name of the Lord is a strong tower; the righteous run to it and are safe"* (Proverbs 18:10). I can absolutely depend on the fact that God is truth. That is a place of strength. It is a fortress. When I am found in that fortress, no enemy or circumstance or crisis or trial can harm me. My security is in God, not myself or my circumstances. These two truths: God loves me and is my hiding place, and God is absolute truth and is my Strong Tower, have become foundations in my life that cannot be shaken.

I read Jeremiah 29:11 over and over again. As I meditated on that verse, I began to see some important phrases found there. These phrases were not just idol words, they were specific things spoken to comfort me and give me a place of peace in the midst of my struggle.

These phrases are:

1. I know the plans I have for you.
2. I have plans to prosper you.
3. I do not plan to harm you.
4. I plan to give you hope.
5. I plan to give you a future.

Let me share with you the impact that each of these phrases had on my life. I have taken comfort in these things over and over again. Before I do that, I must share with you an event that took place one day shortly after my discovery of Jeremiah 29:11. Cathy and I have come to fondly call it:

THE DRIVE

In these early days of the crisis, I was beginning to learn the things I shared above. I understood that God was my Hiding Place and my Strong Tower. Still, I attempted to escape from the daily struggles by getting away from home. Somehow it felt like I was detached from the situation for awhile. But each time I did that, the harsh reality of the circumstance was there waiting for me when I arrived home.

One day I woke up in the morning and decided I wanted to take a day-long drive. I asked Cathy if she would like to go, and soon we were ready and in the car. I planned to go somewhere I had not been before. I was born and raised in the Willamette Valley of Oregon and knew most every community and road. But I discovered an area I had never been. It would be a short drive, easily made in just a few hours there and back.

I have an inexpensive GPS unit in my car. So I punched in the town we were headed for and away we went. I blindly followed the directions my GPS squawked to me. We made all the appropriate turns and soon were beyond any area I had been before. We found ourselves climbing a mountain on a winding road. Although it was beautiful, the road was treacherous and made for very slow going. We finally reached the summit of the mountain and began the descent down the other side. The road was equally treacherous. As we reached the bottom of the mountain, we came around a corner and entered a very small town. This town was literally in the middle of nowhere. We didn't see this coming at all.

The town was so small that only a handful of houses were there. There were no businesses to speak of except for a small gas stop. However, there was one very impressive element to this town. On one side of the road was a very large college campus, complete with dormitories and large classroom pods. There were business offices and a beautiful campus with lush green grass and walking paths that covered all of the grounds. There were large parking lots able to park hundreds of vehicles. As we drove past, we saw a sign at the entrance and discovered that it was a Christian college equipping people for evangelism. This college seemed out of place in this very small town in the country, well off the beaten path.

As we continued the drive, we found that the road became wider, certainly flatter and very straight. It was smooth sailing as we completed our trip to the community we had gone to see. When we made the return trip, we found that there was a road that went around the mountain. This highway was wide and smooth with very few turns. But we had taken a pathway that led us through ups and downs, many curves and treacherous driving.

The drive took most of the day and by evening time we were home again. Cathy and I didn't talk much about it that night. But by the next morning, it certainly was the topic of our conversation.

Both of us had the same revelation about the drive. It was a microcosm of our lives, particularly our Christian lives. As we thought back to the past, we realized that we had been on familiar roads. They were, for the most part, easy to navigate without very many treacherous areas. But God had brought us to a very unfamiliar and seemingly dangerous road. All that we had in our lives that gave us security was gone. We were literally in the hands of God and his mercy to lead us safely through this difficult time. This was like the mountain road.

We also knew that the discovery of the Christian college at the end of the mountain road was beginning to show itself in our lives. Although the going was treacherous, we knew that God was 'taking us back to school' in our relationships with him. He wanted to equip us in new ways and send us off again to face the future.

The promise of the future was also shown during the drive. We found that after we had navigated the mountain road, gone through the town with the Christian college and moved on, the path became smooth and straight. We soon reached our destination. This was the promise we were receiving from God. He truly did have a plan for us and the future was in his hands. The future spoke of straighter paths that would be easier to navigate. There was a clear destination at the end of that path. All the signs pointed to that destination just like the signs on the highway pointed us to the town we were visiting.

It was on that day that we realized God had us in his hands. Our future was not uncertain to him. Although we didn't know what the future held for us, God did, and there was security in that. We saw a glimpse of the possibilities of our future. And the future looked brighter. This helped us put the crisis in perspective. Although the current road was rough and treacherous, God was leading us somewhere. Somewhere that he had planned in advance for us to go.

Now that you have experienced "the drive" along with me, let's look at Jeremiah 29:11 phrase by phrase. These things became life to me as I dealt with my own crisis.

I Know the Plans I Have for You

The security that I had lost was really no security at all. I trusted in the stability of my circumstances rather than in the Strong Tower, Jesus Christ. Circumstances change, trials come and go, and crisis enters lives once in awhile. If I am trusting in my circumstances, I am trusting in something that is movable, changing, and unstable. But if I trust in God, I know that he never changes. He is absolutely stable.

I love this translation of Jeremiah 29:11 (NKJV), *"For I know the thoughts that I think toward you, says the Lord, thoughts of peace and not of evil, to give you a future and a hope."* I know that God created everything with just a word. He spoke and things were created. This gives me new insight into how incredibly great God really is; when he thinks about me, plans are created. My whole life is planned simply because of one thought from God. And he knows those thoughts. He remembers them. Everything that he has laid out for my life is in his thoughts. He never forgets the thoughts he has toward me.

When I realized that the God of the universe had a specific plan for my life, it changed the way I viewed my circumstances. Even though I didn't know what was ahead, he did. That means that everything I experienced in my Christian life to that point had been ordained by him. It also meant that everything that will happen from that time on is also ordained by him. This is where true security is found. The work that had already begun in me, through my faith, was producing a trust in God's ability to rule my life. He had set me on a path. Though I didn't understand, a master plan was in place. He held me in the palm of his hand.

I HAVE PLANS TO PROSPER YOU

It is not easy to see a positive outcome when you are in the midst of a crisis. I could not see an end to the situation I was in. One thing I learned through this time of trial was that if I allowed my emotions to reign, if my own thoughts and ideas about the situation were my guidance, I was doomed to failure. It is hard to be objective when you are in crisis. I found that my emotions were at times out of control. I would feel better about things one moment and in the next, I was buried in a pit of despair.

The truth that God had plans to prosper me was life-changing. The circumstance did not speak of prosperity. It spoke of failure and destruction. But when I exercised my faith to believe what I was reading in the Word and hearing in my spirit, everything changed. God wanted to prosper me. This meant that in every area of my life, spiritual, emotional, physical, financial, relational—everything, God's intent was to prosper me. I thought of the old hymn, "Joyful, Joyful, We Adore Thee." The lyrics say, "Joyful, joyful, we adore thee, God of glory, Lord of love. Hearts unfold like flowers before Thee. Opening to the sun above." The prosperity God was bringing to my life allowed my spirit to unfold before him like a flower opening up to the warmth of the sun. I could receive everything he had for me.

I Do Not Plan to Harm You

In the early days following the dismissal from my job, I often labored under the weight of believing that I was going to be harmed. Finances would fail me. Impending disaster would overtake me. I felt physically ill many times. There were days when I simply wanted to sleep. It was difficult to even rise to face the day. I believed a lie, concocted by the enemy, that my life would only come to a harmful, painful end.

The truth of God's Word set me free from the lies of the enemy. God was speaking to me directly that his intent has never been nor would it ever be to harm me. His plans are to prosper me. He created me and he loves me with an undying, never-ending love. He loves me like his child. He loves me like his bride. He loves me like his brother. He calls me his friend. He would never harm me. Like a parent wants the best for his children, he wants and wills that I prosper and not be harmed.

I Plan to Give You Hope

Hope and dreams—God wanted me to experience those things again. I had lost hope. I was consumed in my circumstance and everything I saw looked hopeless. A middle-aged man looking for a new career looked hopeless. Returning to my former career looked hopeless. But hope is big on God's priority list for us as Christians. 1 Corinthians 13:13 tells us *"And now these three remain: faith, hope and love . But the greatest of these is love."* These are big things on God's mind for us. For me that meant that along with the new faith that was rising up in my life, hope was to be right there as well.

When it comes down to it, hope is simply a change of mindset. I was thinking destructive thoughts and believing the lies of the enemy. God was offering thoughts of prosperity and hope. If I would believe those things and change my mind from the other ways, I would have a whole new outlook. That is exactly what happened. I changed my mind. I chose to believe God's Word and believe that I had hope. I started seeing things from a different perspective. I could see potential that there was an end to the dark tunnel I found myself in. On the other side of my crisis, there was something great waiting for me. It was the opportunity to live in the will of the Father. There is no greater hope. This is a God-sized hope.

I Plan to Give You a Future

I could not see into the future. I had no idea what lay ahead for Cathy and me. But, in an instant, I realized that I had a future. It was not a future of failure or destruction. It was a future that had been planned for me since before the creation of the world. If I had a future, I wasn't going to die. If I had a future, I wasn't going to live in a prison of my own making. If I had a future, God wanted me to be victorious. I had not even thought of a word as bold as "victory" to describe what I was going through or where I was headed. But victory is exactly what God had planned for me.

"The drive" truly was a microcosm of our Christian lives. There was a past and God had directed every step. There is a present and God was directing that path as well. It may have been a climb, a crooked and difficult road, but he was leading us. And most importantly, there is a future. This time of crisis would not last forever, and God had already set the future in motion. I knew that the road would lead me to a place of being with him and learning from him. Then it would widen and become easier to navigate. The key was to allow him to guide my future. Ah, the relief of allowing God to rule my past, present and future! The plan was perfect!

To You, From God

Dear One,

I have spent much time watching you. Although I know the struggle you are going through is difficult and hard to understand, I want to assure you that I have orchestrated everything that has happened in your life. My ways are sometimes difficult for you to comprehend, but I always have your best interest in mind. I love you and everything I do is motivated by that love. You are more precious to me than anything in the universe or the earth. I have placed part of myself in you. You are a very special child.

I am writing because I see the tendency you have to panic about your situation. Although I understand that you cannot see things from my point of view, you can begin to see beyond your circumstance. If you will trust in me and look for the things I have in store for you, you will be absolutely victorious. You will be greater in my kingdom than you have ever imagined. Please do not panic. If you will only spend time with me, I will keep you safe. You will know my *peace that surpasses all understanding.*

I want you to know that I have big plans for you. Before you were even knit together in your mother's womb, my plans were set. I see where you have been, where you are now and where you will go. To me, it is all one picture of your life. People sometimes call this "destiny," but in reality, it is my complete plan for you. If I can comfort you with some words, it would be this: your crisis will not last. It will pass and you will enter into the continuation of my plan for you. Oh, if you could only see what I see! The best days of your life lie ahead.

Sometimes, it is difficult to understand this, but you must know that my intent is never to harm you. I love you so much that I simply cannot bring harm to you. I know that it is an easy trap to fall in, but please don't blame me or be angry at me because of your circumstance. I have already told you that I have orchestrated all that has happened, and all of these things have been done because I have your best interest in my heart. I have spoken the truth when I said, *"Never will I leave you; never will I forsake you."* Of this you can be sure: I am always with you.

Now, for the most exciting part of my letter: I plan to prosper you with an abundance that is beyond your understanding. The kind of prosperity I am speaking of includes your spirit, soul, body, finances, relationships with others, and every possible area of your life. You see, this is how my kingdom operates. No one who is living in my kingdom is wanting for anything. Though you may not understand right now, you will soon know the truth of these words.

Dear one, start to hope again. The plans I have for you include hope. There is no future without hope. There is nothing to look forward to if you don't have hope. I want you to look forward, with anticipation, to the future I have for you. It is a place and time filled with my blessings. Don't be discouraged by the things you see around you right now. Things will change. Keep believing in my plan, hoping for greater things and trusting in me. And one more thing: Don't forget that I love you. Keep listening and I will tell you more.

All my thoughts are on you,
God

7

"I AM HEALING YOU"

Old Questions Answered

"And afterward, I will pour out my Spirit on all people.
Your sons and daughters will prophecy, your old men will
dream dreams, your young men will see visions."

JOEL 2:28

God speaks to us in varieties of ways. One of the ways I have seen and heard direction from God is through dreams. I have seen the evidence of how God uses dreams to communicate with us. The Bible is full of stories in both the Old and New Testaments about times when God changed people's lives, direction, and even the course of nations by revealing his will to people through dreams.

One night many years ago, I had a dream. The next night, it continued. This was a dream that affected me deeply. Even now, after nearly twenty-five years, I remember the pictures with precise clarity. I had thought of it many times over the years, but I never was able to find answers as to its meaning. I had ideas about what God was speaking to me, but somehow it never seemed to be quite right. I believed that this particular dream was about direction for my life and spoke of the future life I would lead for Christ.

Now, in the middle of my personal crisis, the dream would resurface. I had made plans to meet with a friend to discuss the happenings in my life. Michael is a friend that I knew I could say anything to. It didn't matter how I felt, how angry or upset I was. He could handle it and would be there no matter what the issue was. I was very emotional and was still reeling from the events. I knew that this had the potential to be an emotional encounter. We were meeting for lunch in a small restaurant. There were no booths, only tables with no separation between. I hoped I wouldn't make a spectacle of myself for the lunch crowd to see. Fortunately, there were only a few people in the little restaurant and those were seated several tables away from us.

I began to share my predicament with Michael. I was very emotional and fought back tears as I articulated the events leading up to our lunch meeting. He was understanding and asked questions, mostly I think to give me a break from the onslaught of tears and emotion. He asked what my plans were and what he could do to help me in a job search. Suddenly, as he was speaking, my mind was flooded with the memory of the dream. It came so suddenly and strongly that I found it difficult to concentrate on what he was saying. Why would this come to me at this particular moment? I concluded that God had a purpose. I was to tell my dreams to my friend.

Cautiously, I began to recall the dreams that were given to me all those years ago. I remembered the pictures and events and shared them with as much clarity as I could.

In the first dream, I walked up to a construction site. I grew up in the building industry, so this was nothing new to me. This was a large building with a huge concrete floor. The building was several stories tall and had a complicated roof that involved many different small gables, dormers, and other outcroppings. The building was being framed. There was no plywood or sheetrock. It was a mass of sticks of lumber nailed together. There were what appeared to be hundreds of laborers working on the building. Some were nailing lumber in place on the walls. Others were on the roof working. Still others were carrying lumber to different parts of the building. I remember thinking that it looked like a "Waldo" picture. I walked onto the concrete and approached a wooden bench. Sitting on the bench was a man. As I drew near, I recognized the man as a former teacher of mine. I had great respect for this man. Without saying a word, I sat down on the bench next to him. He pointed to a small gable, very high on the roof. It couldn't have been more than four feet long and was very high off the ground. He handed me one small piece of wooden trim and told me that my job was to climb up there and install this one piece. I remember climbing up the side of the building. It took a long time to get up there. When I arrived at the small gable, it was so high off the ground that I was very uncomfortable. I had to adjust and position myself so I felt comfortable working. With that, the dream ended.

The following night, I dreamed again. This time, I was walking to the same building. Everything looked exactly the same. There were hundreds of people working. There was the bench on the concrete floor and my former teacher sitting on it. Again, I approached the bench and quietly sat down beside him. We sat in silence for a short time. Then he turned, looked me in the eye and said, "Barry, do you see all these men working on this building?" I replied, "Yes." He spoke again, "All of these people are not getting the job done. They are not following my instructions. I am going to have to fire all of them. I am going to take all of the jobs they are doing and give them to you. You will take over all their responsibilities. You will replace all of these men. You will finish the building." With those words, the dream ended.

For nearly twenty-five years, I had wondered what those dreams meant. At one time, I thought I understood. I knew I was called into ministry when I was young. I felt that the dreams meant that first I was given a small job to do and after being successful, God would give me greater responsibility in the church. I thought I had experienced some things that seemed to bear that out, but they never quite fit. I never felt I had been given any greater responsibility. The meaning of the dreams had always eluded me.

I shared the dreams with Michael, using the same words I have written here. By this time, we had left the restaurant and had driven the short distance to his place of business. I remember sitting in the car in silence as he thought about the words I had said. I hadn't shared these dreams with any other person except for my wife and family. I felt very vulnerable having opened up a deep area of my life to someone. But I trusted him and waited to hear what he thought.

He asked me if anyone had interpreted the dream for me. Since I had not told many people, the answer was no. He asked if he could tell me what he thought about it. Of course, my answer was yes. I felt that the Lord had brought this to my mind for this moment. There was little question that God had something specific for me. I felt that a defining moment was about to take place. He said that he believed the building in the dream was a picture of my life. The man sitting on the bench was God. My life had been and would continue to be very complex. Like the building, there are many different areas that are being built. Many men and women had input in different areas, but God was bringing me to a point where he would build my life.

Over the next few hours, his interpretation began to make sense. I remembered reading Isaiah 28 (which I wrote about in chapter 2). It was true that many people had influenced my life. They weren't bad people and they had not done harm to me. They simply were not doing the job that God wanted to do. God was bringing me to a point in time when it would be just him and me. He wanted me to be alone with him so he could build his foundation in me. This didn't mean that I was to dismiss all of the things I had learned from people. I simply had to submit those things to God and allow him to place the pieces into the building of my life where he wanted them to go.

This helped define the crisis I was going through. I began to understand that God was going to use this circumstance to strip my life down to just two elements: him and me. Together, we were going to build a solid foundation that was specifically intended for me. His purpose and direction for my life was going to be defined by him, not by other people and certainly not by what I thought. My responsibility was to submit to him and allow him to build me. Then I could enter into the plan he had for me.

It occurred to me that I had responsibility in the building of my life. In the dream, the man (God) told me that all of the other workers would be fired and I was to take all of their responsibilities. That meant that I had to work on my own life. Although I understood God would be the builder, I would have to partner with him, work on my own failings, respond to his voice and obey his direction for my life. It required action on my part. God would provide the direction, and I would make the choices to build my life accordingly.

OVERCOMING FEAR

"For God has not given us a spirit of fear,
but of power and of love and of a sound mind."
2 TIMOTHY 1:7 NKJV

I have read the apostle Paul's letters to Timothy many times. I have always been struck with the notion that there were many things happening in Timothy's life that are not clearly written about, but are evident by reading between the lines. It is obvious to me that Timothy had been through some difficult things. Paul was his spiritual father and knew him well. He had insight into his life that very few others had. As he writes to Timothy, he uses phrases like: *Don't fear, don't be ashamed of the Gospel, I am mindful of your tears, stir up the gift in you, you may be persecuted.* In fact, he mentions that Timothy had some sort of stomach issue. Clearly, he had gone through some difficult things.

Timothy had been hurt somehow. It is not clear what happened. Perhaps it was because he was young and was a spiritual mentor to much older, more mature men. He may have faced rejection because of his age. We will never know in this life what happened to him. But we can be sure of the result. The event or events that caused these issues in Timothy's life left him dealing with an onslaught of fear. I am convinced that it was this fear that prompted Paul to write his second letter. These were words of encouragement to a young man who had faced difficult things and had come out of the circumstance with an overload of fear.

The same fear that had hurt Timothy was now gripping me. It wasn't just this crisis that had left me timid. There had been other events as well. In fact, as I began to honestly look at the role fear was playing in my life, I realized that from the time I was a young boy, I had dealt with it. But it was this point in time, right in the middle of my crisis, when God decided to deal with the deep-seated fear in me.

Three significant things took place during these few days that would revolutionize my life. It is interesting that when a person is gripped and held captive by something as formidable as fear, one simply learns to coexist with it rather than change. I had developed a pattern in my life of simply coping with fear. In doing this, I missed many opportunities afforded to me by God to move into greater things. Some of the things I missed were spiritual blessings, others were financial blessings, and still others were new directions that I could have gone but didn't because of the presence of fear in my life.

The first thing that happened was the exposing of fear. In chapter one, I wrote about my friend and pastor, John. He and his wife, Carol, came to visit us just three days after I was fired from my job. It was an incredible blessing for them to come and minister to us. But even more amazing than the visit was the content of the prayers they prayed over me.

John put his hands on my head and began to pray. As he was praying, he said, "You are bound by fear!" He went on to pray that God would remove fear from me and set me free from its grip. As I mentioned before, there came a release. I could feel that something had happened, but I could not define it. It was simply a feeling of relief and peace that I had not felt for a long time. This was not the kind of prayer I was expecting from him. I was expecting prayers of encouragement, asking God to express his love to me and take care of our needs. Although he did pray those things, the majority of time was spent dealing with the long-standing problem with fear.

I had never considered myself a fearful person. My wife never considered me a fearful person. I have always been a strong husband and father figure. I thought I was on pretty stable ground when it came to fear. However, all I had really done in my life was to bury it inside me. I didn't express it or visibly manifest its stronghold. Fear lay hidden inside of me. It didn't have to be public. Its grip was keeping me from entering into God's blessings. I had learned to live with it. Never had I realized that it was possible to live without it.

This was the day of exposure. No longer could fear lie deep inside of me unnoticed. It had been defined and confronted. Now I was very aware of its influence. I could see it, but I didn't know what to do about it. I didn't know any other way to live. So I began to pray and ask God to help me overcome my fear. When I began to pray, it seemed as if things became worse. I was fearful every time the phone rang. I was afraid to go get the mail. I was afraid when someone knocked on the door. I was simply cowering under the weight of fear. I thought that something else was about to go wrong. My world was falling apart around me.

I began to understand something significant. When fear was left hidden in my life, God and I could not deal with it. Now that it was exposed, we could make progress. I remember a time at my place of business. There was an awful smell in the building. It smelled like something was dead, but we could not find any source. After awhile, during the course of the workday, we got used to the smell and didn't even notice. But the next morning when we came in, it was even worse. We began to aggressively search the building for the culprit.

Later that day, we discovered that a mouse had gotten into a heat duct
that was attached to the furnace. Apparently he couldn't get out again
and died. We found the mouse and we were able to dispose of it. Of
course, the smell was still there and we lived with it for the rest of the
day. The next day, however, the smell was gone and things returned
to normal. This was the process that was about to take place in me.
The source of the issues in my life had been exposed, the mouse had
been found. Now it could be thrown out to allow the fresh, cleansing
breeze of the Holy Spirit to fill my life. Now that it was exposed, it
was manifested by my fear of answering the phone, getting the mail,
or answering the doorbell. These were things I could deal with. And
I did. I began to apply the Word of God to those thoughts. I would
take them captive and make them obedient to Christ. *"But everything
exposed by the light becomes visible, for it is light that makes everything
visible"* (Ephesians 5:13-14). Fear could not hide itself from the purity
of God's light.

I mentioned that fear had gripped me from a young age. During
these few days of my crisis, I remembered a situation that happened
when I was fourteen years old. I had just entered my freshman year of
high school. At this age, I had grown to my adult size. I was athletic
and physically big enough to take on high school athletics. It was
football season and it soon became evident to the coaches that I was
able to play at a varsity level. No freshman had received their varsity
letter in football in the history of our school. But I found myself playing more and more through the first several games of the season.

Our football team was very good. We were ranked in the top five
in the state. Our first league football game was to be with a school
that was ranked number one. The game was on their home field.
We prepared well and made the trip that early October night to the
opposing school. We dressed in the locker room as usual. Every player
had different ways of preparing for the game. Some would sit quietly
and not speak even if spoken to. Some would pace the locker room.

Others would be jovial, joking with teammates. But, this night, everyone in the locker room knew that this game would decide the state champion at the end of the year.

When we ran onto the field that night, I had never seen so many people attending a high school football game. They were lined around the entire field with all of the grandstands filled beyond capacity. I had played in football games before, but this one was different. This one was huge. I was immediately intimidated. Through the entire first half of the game, I didn't play. The coaches didn't call my name and I was fine with that. At half time, the score was 13 to 7. The other team was ahead.

At halftime, the coach gave his usual motivational speech. This one was more fiery than most. We were used to being ahead at the half, not trailing. We were almost ready to run back onto the field when the coach approached me and said, "Barry, you be ready to go in this half. You will be playing." I was immediately afraid. We ran back on the field and played the second half. For the rest of the game, I hid myself from the coach. That is relatively easy to do when there are sixty players plus coaches and staff standing on the sidelines. We finished the game, losing 13 to 7 after being stopped on the one-yard line near the end of the fourth quarter. I never played at all.

The Lord reminded me of this incident. To me it was a vivid reminder that I had always lived in fear. I was physically equipped to play in that game. I had been prepared by the coaches to play. But when it came time to actually do what I was prepared to do, I hid in fear. I had an opportunity to make a difference. Instead, I ran away. With this memory came a new resolve in me. I was ready to deal with fear once and for all. I had been held captive long enough. It was time to be free.

I mentioned my issues with fear to a close friend. He said something to me that I will never forget. He said, "Fear cripples you." This was absolutely true. I had been crippled by fear and for that reason was unable to enter into the blessings God had for me.

All this information now flooded my soul. God, who is always on time, showed up again. I had another dream. It was obvious that God was dealing with this crippling fear. In this dream, I was walking alongside a tall wall. It was, as I imagined, like the wall of an ancient city. I was at one end of it and it stretched as far as the eye could see. In front of it was something that looked like a planter box. It also ran as far as the wall did and was attached to it. It looked like something a person would plant flowers or other plants in, but this one had planted in it the heads of men. Literally, it was as if someone had cut off the heads of men and placed them in the planter. I walked the full length of the wall until I reached the other end. There was a man there and he was fishing with his hands in a large barrel filled with serpents. As he fished, he spoke to me. He said, "All of the kings who came before are nothing compared to this one. This one is a thousand times more powerful." With those words, I awoke. It was morning.

When I awoke, there was a phrase in my mind immediately. The phrase was, "Kill the king." I pondered this dream for the next day. It was disturbing, yet I was sure it was given to me by God. I prayed and asked for the wisdom to understand what was being said. Suddenly, as if it were simply inserted into my thoughts, the answer came. I knew that the wall was my life. I had walked it from beginning to the point in time where I was now. The planter that was filled with the heads of kings represented all of the sin and evil influences in my life that God had slain. The king that I was now facing, the one that was a thousand times more powerful than any of the others, was fear. And the mandate from God was clear; "Kill the king."

I began to aggressively pray for answers. I realized that the enemy of faith is fear. Fear is the polar opposite of faith. I knew that I could not live in faith if I continued to submit to fear. So I began to exercise my faith. I have written earlier about faith. The message had already been presented to me and it required action in order to be faith at all. So I started to act. I bravely retrieved the mail, answered the phone and the door. These may seem like small things, but to me these were breakthroughs. Then I began to act on things I believed the Lord was speaking to me or the evidence of things I saw. This opened up a new lifestyle for me, one without fear always nagging at me. I simply did the things I felt I was supposed to do without regard for the consequences. It didn't matter to me if I were rejected or if it didn't go quite right. I was fulfilling my faith through obedience. Fear was no longer in the equation. It was liberating.

Let me share one final thought regarding this monumental time in my life. I remember thinking about the word, "fearless." I had always thought that a person who was fearless was a daredevil. This was the kind of person who would jump his motorcycle over a canyon or high dive off of a cliff into the ocean. That was not me. Then I realized that the word fearless, when broken down simply means 'fear less.' I didn't have to be a daredevil to be fearless. All I had to do was exercise faith and be obedient to God without fear. I could do that; I was doing that. I was slaying the king of fear and my life was changing.

Some Words for You

I have shared some personal and intimate things that have occurred in my life and in my relationship with Jesus. These are things that have not been made public before. So, why now, why share them with you? There is only one answer: I want you to understand that the same kinds of miraculous breakthroughs I have experienced are possible for you.

I understand what it is like to go through a life crisis. I have been there. While my crisis was raging, I made a choice to allow God to do anything he wanted in me. For me the choice was simple and I had nothing else to lose. I wanted change so desperately that I was willing to allow God to literally tear down my life and rebuild it his way.

You may be going through your own crisis. You may be reading this simply because it looked interesting or because you know someone who is in a crisis. Whatever the case, God wants to change you. He wants to defeat things in your life that keep you from entering into all the blessings and adventures he has for you. I cannot express in words how incredible it is to live without being bound by fear. For me, this was a destiny changing moment. No longer was I destined to live a spiritual life of mediocrity. Now I could live in the greatness that God had ordained for me.

In the Old Testament, we read about many great events that happened to God's chosen people, the Israelites. Every time God did something significant, a miracle or other great event, they would build an altar there. This was done so the event would never be forgotten. Even future generations would walk by the altar and remember what God had done for their forefathers. Some of those altars exist today.

It is of utmost importance that we "build altars" in our lives. You may remember something significant that God said or did for you somewhere along the path of your Christian life. Remember it. Write it down and think of it often. I keep a journal and look back often to remember the things God did for me. This writing is a result of doing just that. God can bring back something as memorable as a dream or as seemingly insignificant as a high school football game. He will use these things to bring his revelation to our lives. And he will do it at just the right moment. Brothers and sisters, always remember what God has done for you and said to you.

If there are major obstacles in your spiritual life to overcome, allow God to dissect your life. My obstacle was fear. God faithfully brought it to the surface and allowed me through his grace to deal with it. He will do the same for you. A time of crisis need not be simply a time for surviving. It can be a pathway to an overcoming victory for you.

Rend your heart

and not your garments.
Return to the LORD your God,
for he is gracious and compassionate,
slow to anger and abounding in love,
and he relents from sending calamity." Joel 2:13

The process of rending can be painful. The word, "rend" literally means *'to violently tear apart.'* It is not easy to tear open your heart before God and allow him to change it. But if you will do just that, it will be the most rewarding thing you will ever do. Your destiny will be changed forever.

Finally, you may relate to the story about the high school football game. If you are hiding from God and not allowing him to deal with the internal struggles of your life, make a decision to stand firmly right beside him. Allow him to deal with your life and use you in whatever capacity he chooses. I did that and now instead of hiding from him, I go where he goes. I stand ready for him to use me. I say to him, "Here I am, send me, use me. Put me in the game. I am ready." If you will do that, God will defeat the "kings" in your life. And he will use you to do his will.

8

"I HAVE KEYS FOR YOU"

An Encounter with God

"I will give you the keys of the kingdom of heaven."

MATTHEW 16:19

The most significant moment in my spiritual life happened one Saturday morning during the heat of my crisis. I suppose it sounds overdramatic to say that, but it is the truth. Looking back, the only greater experience I have had with God was the day I accepted him and gave my life to him. That day launched me into my spiritual life journey. This encounter was a divine meeting and would change my life. In fact, I often jokingly refer to it as "the day I was saved." This day changed my perspective about the crisis and my life in the kingdom of God.

There were many nights when I didn't sleep well. I had gotten used to that. Volumes of thoughts were still bombarding me. Even at night, it was difficult to avoid. So I woke up early that Saturday morning. As soon as I opened my eyes, there was a phrase in my mind. This was the Holy Spirit speaking to me and I knew it. The phrase was, "I will give you the keys of the kingdom." I knew this was a Bible verse and I had read it before, but I had no idea where it was found. I went and found my Bible concordance and looked up the phrase. I discovered that it was Matthew 16:19. So I sat down on the couch and began to read. No one else had stirred yet, so all was quiet.

Allow me to paraphrase the story found in Matthew 16:13-19. Jesus was with his disciples one day in a place called Caesarea Philippi. He asked the men, "Who do people say that I am?" The disciples answered him, saying, "Some say you are John the Baptist. Some say you are Elijah, and still others say you are Jeremiah or one of the other prophets." At this point, Jesus asked a direct and poignant question; "What about you? Who do you say that I am?" Simon Peter replied, "You are the Christ, the Son of the living God." This is often referred to as "The Good Confession." But the dialogue continues. Jesus said, "You are blessed, Simon, for this was not revealed to you by man, but by my Father in heaven. And I tell you that you are Peter and on this rock, I will build my church and the gates of hell will not prevail against it." At this point, I could see Peter's pride swelling. He must have been thinking what a great thing this was that he would be the foundation of the church. However, he misunderstood what Jesus said. The *rock* he spoke of was the confession of Peter, not the person. The foundation of the church is Jesus and our confession of the Christ is the rock on which the church stands. He made this point here because Peter's confession would become the pattern for every person to receive Christ and join his church. But there was still more Jesus needed to say to him; "Peter, I will give you the keys of the kingdom of heaven; whatever you bind on earth will be bound in heaven, and whatever you loose on earth will be loosed in heaven." This statement gave the disciples much to ponder. It gave me much to think about, too.

I could sense that God wanted to establish something very significant in me. As I meditated, a light came on in my mind. I was drawn to the phrase when Jesus said, "You are blessed Simon, because this was not revealed to you by men, but by my Father in heaven." For the first time, I understood what was so significant to Peter that day. When he said, "You are the Christ, the Son of the living God," he spoke something that was in his heart. It wasn't just something he knew because he heard about it. He knew it in his innermost being. That is what made this the good confession. Actually, you could say Peter was the first convert. He believed in his heart that Jesus was the Christ and he confessed it with his mouth! I had received Christ into my life many years before, but this was something fresh and new for me.

God was continuing to build his new foundation in me. I wept as I realized that I had allowed things that men had taught me to be the foundation of my faith. I was reminded of this scripture: *"Yet I hold this against you: You have forsaken your first love. Remember the height from which you have fallen! Repent and do the things you did at first"* (Revelation 2:4-5).

This was an incredible release. I did remember the things I did at first. I remembered being so in love with Jesus that I talked to him about everything. I remembered childlike faith when I would ask him to make the wind blow . . . and I knew he would do it. I remembered the fire of the Holy Spirit that was in me. Nothing could make me waiver. I was excited about Jesus. Now he was calling me back to that kind of relationship with him. Like Peter, I knew in my heart again that Jesus was the Christ, the Son of the living God. He was alive in me!

It is difficult to convey to you the excitement I felt that morning. I found that it was difficult to share this with my family as well. But I found a way that helped me explain the change in my spirit that occurred that day.

I have a theater room in my house. One of the things that drew me to our house when we were searching for a new home was this house had a large room upstairs that could be a bedroom, but was much larger than all the rest. So I got the idea to make it into a theater. I purchased a projector and a nine-foot screen. I bought a home theater sound system and mounted all the speakers on the wall. I decorated it like a movie theater, complete with framed movie posters, popcorn machine, and even theater seats that I purchased secondhand. I loved this room simply because I had done the work myself and it was a great place to get away. The sound of the movies was amazing. But as I was doing some research about the new technology of digital sound, I discovered that my equipment was capable of this new technology, but I did not have the digital cable that was necessary. So I went down to the local electronic store, purchased the cable and installed it. When I turned the system on, immediately, new lights displayed that I had never seen before. The amplifier lit up and flashed new information. When I played a movie, the sound was incredible. All of the electronic equipment was communicating digitally and reading the exact information that was placed on the DVD. It was an amazing difference.

I used this illustration to share with my family the change that had happened in me. It was literally as if my spirit woke up. I felt a new kind of communication with the Holy Spirit. My mind was enlightened, my prayers changed and there was a new excitement that was greater than anything I had ever experienced. All this happened simply because God revealed to me what Peter felt that day over two thousand years ago. I had a brand new relationship with Jesus.

I had a long and tearful conversation with God that morning. The tears were simply an outpouring of emotion. I had to express to him what I was feeling in my heart. This was another turning point in my crisis. But it was bigger than that. It was a turning point in my spiritual life. I had a new desire to communicate with God. I felt as if he were standing right there talking to me and listening to what I had to say.

As I was praying, I saw a vision. I saw this with my spiritual eyes and it played out in my mind. I saw a river, but it was not flowing. It had logs, pieces of wood, stumps and other debris clogging the flow of the river. Behind it, the river was flowing, but when it reached this wide area, it stopped because of the debris. As I watched, I saw one very large stump begin to dislodge. It slowly moved and water began to fill the area around it. As the pressure of the water increased, other pieces of wood, logs and limbs began to dislodge as well. Soon these things were all swept up in the current of the river that was now flowing through the area. Before the vision ended, the area was emptied of the obstructions and the river was raging through without interruption.

This was a vision illustrating what had just happened in my life. Many of the things that had been deposited in me were not the life-flowing river of God. They were just obstructions to his work in me. I had placed these things there myself. Some were the result of sin that had gone unchecked. Others were ideas about God and his kingdom that just weren't accurate. I had believed some lies from the enemy that tainted my image of God and how his kingdom works. But in one short experience, one encounter, God exposed all of those things and washed them away in the cleansing flood of Jesus. The slate was cleared. My spirit was opened to receive all the life that the Son had for me.

THE KINGDOM OF HEAVEN

I began to meditate on the phrase the Lord had given me: *"I will give you the keys of the kingdom."* It occurred to me that I had little to no comprehension of the kingdom of Heaven. What is it? What does it have to do with my life? I have to tell you that since that day, the Lord has revealed much to me about his kingdom. In fact, he has shown me much more than I am able to share here. But what I learned in the few days following my experience with him opened up a new and exciting facet of my relationship with God. Allow me to share just five scriptures the Lord showed me regarding his kingdom. Each spoke a new truth to me that I had not understood previously.

"But seek first his kingdom and his righteousness, and all these things will be given to you as well" (Matthew 6:33). In this portion of Matthew 6, Jesus was teaching the people to not be so concerned about

the necessities of life. He told them to not pay so much attention to what they would eat or drink or what clothes they would wear. He said that the lilies that grow in the field do not worry about such things; why should they? I knew this scripture and I knew the context in which it was written. But applying the truth of this statement always eluded me. It seemed that I could not help myself; I had to worry. I had always worried about whether we would have enough money. I worried about providing an adequate home for my family. I knew that Jesus was telling the people not to worry. So what was the problem, why could I not stop?

The reality was I was not seeking the kingdom of God (the phrase, "kingdom of heaven" and the phrase, "kingdom of God," are used interchangeably in the Gospels). I had always tried to seek God and allow him to provide for me, but I continued to undermine the process by worrying about the physical needs of my life.

The first step was to understand what the kingdom of God is. His kingdom is in the unseen world. It lies in the heavenly realms. It is not discernable through the familiar senses we have: sight, hearing, taste, smell and touch. It is, in fact, spiritually discerned. So the first thing I needed to do was engage my spiritual senses to experience his kingdom. His kingdom is vast. It is amply supplied with everything I need. Its bounty is available to all Christians. His kingdom has everything I need to live. This wonderful spiritual life spills over into the physical realm, but the key is to seek the kingdom.

I believed in the kingdom of God; I even thought I was obeying this scripture by seeking after it. But I continued to focus on the physical things: money, clothing, food, etc. I felt that the kingdom was simply a pathway to all my needs being met. My focus was wrong. So I implemented a new strategy. I determined to seek God and his kingdom *instead* of using it as a way to meet my needs. Matthew 6:33 is very clear. We are to seek the kingdom instead of seeking the daily provision for our lives. I determined to stop worrying about the physical things and start learning about the spiritual ones. I learned that every-thing I need is found in his kingdom. This gave me a new perspective. I stopped dwelling on the difficulties I was facing in the physical realm and started looking through my spiritual eyes. There I saw an exciting adventure waiting for me, discovering the kingdom of heaven.

These words are familiar to people all over the world:

This, then, is how you should pray:
Our father in heaven,
hallowed be your name,
your kingdom come,
your will be done on earth as it is in heaven. Matthew 6:9-10

This comes from the passage of scripture we often call, "The Lord's Prayer." Jesus was teaching the people how they should pray. He instructed them to tell God to bring his kingdom to the earth. As I read the entire prayer, I noticed that Jesus did not instruct the people to ask God for anything. This prayer is about declaring to God what we would like him to do. There is no pleading, no weakly worded phrases. This prayer is forceful, it is powerful.

Something new was being revealed to me. I could literally ask God to bring his kingdom into my world. I could do this because it has already been established in the spiritual world. I began to pray this way, "Lord, let your kingdom be established in my life as it is already established in heaven." As I prayed this, it became easier to focus on the kingdom and not my problems and circumstance. New spiritual insights came as I began to experience more of the abun-dance of the kingdom.

A portion of the kingdom of God has been deposited in each one who has received Christ. Luke 17:21 says, *"The kingdom of God is within you."* I came to realize that it is in me because the Holy Spirit lives in me. He is the portion of the kingdom that has been given to each of us. Because this is true, I have access to the kingdom of God all the time. There is never a moment that I am without the Holy Spirit. He is the embodiment of God's kingdom in me.

We read in Matthew 11:12: *"From the days of John the Baptist until now, the kingdom of heaven has been forcefully advancing, and forceful men lay hold of it."* To understand God's kingdom, I had to understand the principle of multiplication. The kingdom is advancing so rapidly that it is exponentially multiplying. As more and more people have become Christians over the generations, it is deposited in them. God's kingdom never runs out. It has no limits. It is infinite in its scope, its power and its resources. This is a concept that is very difficult to understand. My mind is limited and I cannot grasp the immenseness of it all. One scripture comes to mind to explain:

> *And I pray that you, being rooted and established in love, may have power, together with all the saints, to grasp how wide and long and high and deep is the love of Christ, and to know this love that surpasses knowledge-that you may be filled to the measure of all the fullness of God.* Ephesians 3:17b-19

Although it is not possible for me to fully understand God's kingdom and the incredible love of Christ, it is my mission in life to grasp it.

I had always been curious about Matthew 11:12. Each time I read the verse I identified with it and felt that it was something very important for my life. But I didn't understand the message, because I had not understood the kingdom. When I was awakened to the reality of the kingdom, I wanted it in my life. I saw the potential and the power to change me. I desired the kingdom so much that I was willing to be forceful to receive it.

Jesus often spoke of the kingdom. Many times he used parables to describe it to the disciples and other followers. In one of those word pictures, he described the kingdom as something valuable. He said it is like a man who after years of searching found a pearl of tremendous value. When he found it, he went and sold everything he had so he could purchase it. When I began to see the kingdom as more valuable than anything else, I found myself willing to give up everything to obtain it.

Romans 14:17 says, *"For the kingdom of God is not a matter of eating and drinking, but of righteousness, peace and joy in the Holy Spirit."* Too long I had lived my Christian life in the flesh. I had bought into the idea of religion with all its legalistic values. In the long run, these things proved to be without depth. I could not attain a growing relationship with Jesus through the careful observance of mandated rules.

I found liberty in my life through an understanding of the kingdom of God. The joy of living in the kingdom is found in the fact that the Holy Spirit lives in me. When I looked at the things Jesus said about the Holy Spirit, I began to understand the freedom that was available. Jesus said the Holy Spirit would be sent in his name. He said he would be our Comforter, our Counselor. The Spirit brings all things to our remembrance. He leads us into all truth. When I realized that relationship was already in existence in me, I knew I was free to live in and enjoy the kingdom. You see, this verse tells me not to depend on the physical part of my life, but instead to depend on the righteousness, peace, and joy that are resident in me through the Holy Spirit. I still pray daily asking God to give me righteousness, peace, and joy in the Holy Spirit.

Let's look back at 1 Corinthians 4:20: *"For the kingdom of God is not a matter of talk but of power."* In my Christian life, I spent a lot of time talking. I taught regularly and I was a pastor for several years. I was used to talking to groups. I was used to teaching about God and our relationships with him. But I had missed this truth—the kingdom is about power, not just talk. The power of the kingdom must be evident in me. Jesus said that you know if a tree is good by its fruit. If it has good fruit, it is a good tree. If it has bitter fruit or no fruit, it is a bad tree. This is a simple thing to understand. When I applied that to my own life, I realized that the things I have spoken or written must be evident in my own life as the power of the Holy Spirit. If it isn't, I am simply speaking and writing empty things with no value.

When I read this verse, other things began to make sense to me. I had read in the Bible that I am to be filled with the Holy Spirit. I read that I am to walk with the Holy Spirit and keep in step with him. I read stories about how the early church was empowered by him. Through that strength, the blind saw, the deaf heard, the lame walked, and the dead were raised to life. The church was scattered across the known world and established in power. These were all things I knew, but had not been practicing in my own life. It was absolutely necessary for me to recognize every moment that I am partnered with the Holy Spirit. This is the power of the kingdom of God. When I realized that, the kingdom began to be manifested in me. I prayed in faith, my life began to change, and I knew that not only would I survive the crisis, I would be victorious!

What Are the Keys of the Kingdom?

The promise I received that day was; "I will give you the keys of the kingdom." In the days that followed, I learned about the kingdom. I understood it better and began to see it operate in my life. But what are the keys? To answer that question, I thought I would start with the basics. What is a key and what does it do? A key is a device that opens locked places. It gives access to areas that are otherwise inaccessible. A key is made specifically for a certain lock. It matches that lock perfectly. Keys allow automobiles, tractors, and other equipment to operate and do the work they were made to do. If there are no keys, the equipment is simply an immovable piece of metal. Keys are important. I could not function in the world if I did not have keys. The same is true in the spiritual world. If there are no keys, there is no access. There is no power to move things. So it is clear that I had to have keys to access the kingdom.

Keys that do not match a lock are worthless. In my house, I have a lot of keys that don't seem to fit anything. I always say, "I better not throw them away. Someday I will find what lock they go with." The same is true of spiritual keys. If we know the Bible but never exercise or implement the things written there, we have keys that are worthless. They won't unlock anything in the kingdom of heaven. We must know the spiritual keys and know how and where to use them to access the areas of the kingdom that we need.

I have read some Bible commentaries that attempt to explain what Jesus told Peter; "I will give you the keys of the kingdom." Many of them believe that Jesus was giving Peter keys that no one else except the apostles could ever have. They say that the keys of the kingdom ended with the deaths of those men. How shortsighted this is! If the keys of the kingdom are not available to you and me, what hope is there for us to live a victorious spiritual life? God was promising me the keys and I knew it. It didn't matter what the commentators said.

God revealed to me some things about the keys. First, he says, "keys" (plural) not "key" (singular). I have more than one key. There are different keys to access different areas of the kingdom. There are keys that make things work. So I asked God what my keys were.

For me, I knew that one key is prayer. I have been called to be a praying man. Of all the things I have done or ever will do for God, none will be greater than the prayers I bring before him. That is a key of the kingdom in my life. Another is faith. I have already written about the revolutionizing of my faith. Fear had disappeared and I had full access through my faith to the kingdom. I remembered that simply believing in the kingdom was not enough. I had to act on that belief and enter into it. Other keys in me have to do with the gifting the Lord has given me. I know that he gave these abilities to me because I am to use them for the furthering of the kingdom. They are to be used to bring it into my life so I can give it away to others. The keys are different for different people. What your keys are may be different than mine. But there is one key that is critical for all of us to access the kingdom in all its fullness.

The Word of God is the manifestation of God himself. When I read the Bible, it is a reflection of God. Everything in his character is written in those words. Those words penetrate my life and separate spirit and soul, even joints and marrow. The Bible tells me that everything I need for life and godliness is found in its content. It says that I need to hide those words in my heart so I won't sin against God. David said,

> *Then my enemies will turn back*
> *when I call for help.*
> *By this I will know that God is for me.*
> *In God whose word I praise, in the LORD whose word I praise."*
> Psalm 56:9-10

David understood that God and his Word cannot be separated. If I hide God's Word in my heart, I know God.

SOME WORDS FOR YOU

We all need to experience God. I had an experience with him that led me into a deeper relationship. You may not have the same experience I did. I had an encounter that was necessary to move me into position to experience him. If you are in crisis, position yourself to experience God. Although this may sound elementary, the way we do that is by reading the Word and praying. When I was in crisis, it sometimes took all the strength I had to read the Word or pray. But it was what got me through and led to victory through the circumstance.

In order to experience the kingdom of God, you must know the King. If you don't have a growing relationship with him, set yourself to get one. If you have been a Christian for a long time, as I have, take the opportunity to have a fresh encounter with God. When you are honest with him, he will be honest with you. And when he expresses that honesty to you, he always does it in love. We don't have to fear an encounter with God. We should, instead, anticipate it with enthusiasm.

Listen carefully to the things the Lord may speak to you. I have learned through many years of relationship with him how to hear his voice. There are occasions when I miss it. But he is faithful to speak again in ways I will hear and understand. He does this for you as well. Don't discount dreams, visions, or thoughts that may be God's voice in you. Hearing is an automatic function. When someone speaks, we hear it because we are equipped to do so. However, listening requires an intention to hear, receive, and process what is being spoken. If you listen, you will hear a wealth of encouragement, direction, and instruction from the Holy Spirit.

Begin to seek the kingdom. If you will apply Matthew 6:33 to your daily life, it will revolutionize your experience. Your crisis will become less consuming and your spiritual eyes will be opened to a new world of blessing. God knows your crisis. He knows exactly what you are going through. His desire is for you to begin to see it through his eyes. When you begin to experience that, your perspective will change. The things that used to be important won't be any longer. And those spiritual insights that eluded you in the past will come in waves over your spirit.

Jesus told Peter he would give him the keys of the kingdom. He told me he would give them to me as well. That same word from God is for you. Have no doubt that his desire is for you to have the keys of the kingdom. In fact, he is offering them as a gift to you. Have you ever received a wrapped gift and not opened it? Of course not! When you receive a gift, you want to know exactly what is inside. Take this approach to find out what your keys are.

Use the key that is given to all of us. Read the Word of God. There is no amount of scriptures that you must read daily. Some days, you may only read a chapter or a few verses. Other days, you may find time to read more. But it is the same Holy Spirit who reveals the things of the kingdom no matter how much or how little you read. God's Word is him. If you know his living Word, you know him. Hebrews 4:12 tells us that his word is sharper than a two-edged sword. It is a weapon used to defeat the enemy and our flesh. Take up that weapon so that you can stand firm. Then use it to advance into the kingdom. Be forceful, be militant. Be adventurous. Make Bible reading a priority each day. Do this, and your perspective of crisis will change.

9

"I AM RESTORING YOU"

The Restoration Process

"Simon son of John, do you truly love me more than these?"

JOHN 21:15

I have said previously that I relate to Simon Peter. I found that during my crisis time, I related to him as Peter the disciple. It seems that he underwent the entire spectrum of emotions during his time with Jesus. There was the time when Jesus washed the disciples' feet. Peter refused to allow it, saying that Jesus should not be humbling himself to wash his feet. Then, after Jesus explained that if he did not allow it, he would have no part in his kingdom, he exclaimed, *"Then Lord, not just my feet, but my hands and my head as well!"* (John 13:9). Peter was emotional. He was daring and it often got him in trouble.

There are many stories I could tell about Peter and his life as a disciple of Jesus. Many of them you would know well. But I want to focus on one area of Peter's story. It begins as he is forced to deal with the capture, trial, and crucifixion of Jesus and ends less than two months later. This story deals with a tremendous failure. But the great thing about being a follower of Jesus is that he never leaves us in our failures. He restores and makes us even greater in his kingdom. That is exactly what happened to Peter.

I became interested in Peter's story of restoration through a message I heard one Sunday morning. My son-in-law and daughter are children's pastors at a church in another city. We had gone to a service there to witness my little grandson's dedication. I did not know that there would be a message spoken that day that applied directly to my life.

The speaker began to tell the story of Peter. He told how Peter had denied that he knew Jesus on the night before his crucifixion. Later there is a wonderful story of his reconciliation with Jesus and finally, the dramatic change that took place on the day of Pentecost in the second chapter of Acts. That day, I decided that I was going to learn about this story and find out what God was saying to me. Something resonated within me. I could sense that God had a restoration process in place for me just as he had with Peter.

Let's start Peter's story on the night before Jesus's crucifixion. He had had many victorious experiences with Jesus. He was the only one who would dare to walk on the water with Jesus. He was one of the three disciples, along with James and John, who were considered the closest to him. He had made the good confession. These were wonderful things, but he was about to face his darkest hour. After the last supper, Jesus told him that he would deny him three times before the rooster crowed. Peter was appalled. He said he would never deny Jesus. But now in the time of difficulty, he did exactly what was prophesied. When asked if he knew Jesus, he denied it three times. He hung his head in shame when he heard the rooster crow.

The story continues in John 21. Peter was still distraught. Finally, he told the other disciples that he was going to go fishing. This is significant. When Peter was at his lowest point, he went back to what he knew. He was a fisherman before he met Jesus and he thought the best course of action was to go back to his previous occupation, fishing. The other disciples decided they would go with him. After an entire night of fishing, they had caught absolutely nothing. Then, when Peter least expected it, the restoration process began.

Jesus appeared on the shore of the lake. He called to the fishermen and asked them if they had caught any fish. They reported their poor fortune, not knowing that it was Jesus to whom they were speaking. They were told to cast the net on the other side of the boat. When they did, they caught more fish than their nets could possibly hold. They rowed back toward the shore with the nets still in the water. As they approached, they saw that the man they had been talking to was Jesus. Peter, displaying his usual enthusiasm, jumped in the water and swam to Jesus.

Jesus cooked breakfast for them. But his purpose that day was not simply to serve a meal to a group of hungry fishermen. It was to accomplish some eternal business with Peter. He wanted reconciliation. Here is the account of that conversation:

> *When they had finished eating, Jesus said to Simon Peter, "Simon, son of John, do you truly love me more than these?"*
> *"Yes, Lord," he said, "you know that I love you."*
> *Jesus said, "Feed my lambs."*
> *Again, Jesus said, "Simon son of John, do you truly love me?"*
> *He answered, "Yes, Lord, you know that I love you."*
> *Jesus said, "Take care of my sheep."*
> *The third time he said to him, "Simon son of John, do you love me?"*
> *Peter was hurt because Jesus had asked him the third time, "Do you love me?" He said, "Lord, you know all things. You know that I love you."*
> *Jesus said, "Feed my sheep. I tell you the truth, when you were younger you dressed yourself and went where you wanted; but when you are old you will stretch out your hands, and someone else will dress you and lead you where you do not want to go." Jesus said this to indicate the kind of death by which Peter would glorify God. Then he said to him, "Follow me!" Peter turned . . . John 21:15-20*

It is interesting that Peter denied Jesus three times. In this confrontation with him, three times he was asked if he loved him. But

most significant in this exchange were two of Peter's responses. Jesus
initiated this conversation in the hope that Peter would indeed be
responsive and set himself again in right standing with him. Peter's
first significant response was *hurt*. Three times, Jesus had asked him
the same question. The third time, he was hurt. Why did Jesus keep
asking him if he loved him? Even during that night when he denied
knowing him, he still loved him. I believe Jesus asked that question
three times to bring Peter to the place where he would feel hurt. The
second response is found in the last verse, *"Peter turned."* It was necessary to turn around from the direction he was going. Remember that
just a few hours earlier, he had decided to return to his old life and
simply go fishing. Now he was confronted by his Master and brought
to a place of hurt within. After asking him three times if he loved
him, Jesus, knowing that Peter had felt the hurt in his life, said, *"Follow me."* Peter did an about face from the direction he was headed just
a short time earlier and made the decision to turn and follow Christ.

Peter, once again, was laying the foundation for all of us to follow.
He had already shown us the foundation of salvation when he made
the "Good Confession." Now he was showing us the incredible blessing of reconciliation with Christ through repentance.

The apostle Paul later spoke of the need for repentance. He had
written some harsh words to the Corinthian church due to sin that
they continued to participate in. These words were difficult for them
to receive. Apparently it had caused some deep sorrow in them. Yet
Paul stood his ground understanding that this sorrow they felt, just
as Peter had, would ultimately lead them to change their minds about
the sin and complete their repentance: *"Yet now I am happy, not because
you were made sorry, but because your sorrow led you to repentance"* (2
Corinthians 7:9). 'Repentance' literally means, *to change one's mind.*
The act of repentance always consists of the same two elements that
Peter modeled when confronted by Jesus; godly sorrow and turning
away from sin.

Let's pause our story about Peter for a moment so I can tell you
how the things we've looked at affected my life. Unlike him, I had
never denied Christ. From the first day of my salvation, I had always
been a follower of Christ. But like Peter, I had lost some focus and had
gone back to some of the things I had depended on earlier in my life.
I had spent several years being more concerned with making money
and acquiring things than with my relationship with God. During
this time, I did not lose my salvation. I continued to attend church
and be involved in several ministries. But my priority was not my
Christian experience, it was instead the attaining of earthly things. I
know that having earthly things is not wrong. I believe God provides
those things for us, but my priorities were wrong. The things of this
world had become too important to me. I needed to turn around and
follow Christ with all my heart.

Now, through a crisis in my life, Jesus was confronting me in the
same way he did Peter. What choice would I make? Was I willing to
forsake all of the earthly things I had to follow Christ? Jesus was asking me, just as he asked Peter, if I truly loved him. The answer was yes.
So the command was, *"Follow me."* I underwent a change of mind.
My priority shifted. Amidst all the things God was doing in my life,
this was very significant because I initiated change in my own heart.
This was a complete turnaround for me. As I wrote earlier, God had
clearly shown me the necessity of repentance. I was practicing repent-
ing daily. But this was big. I had answered the call to follow Jesus and
forsake my desire to attain worldly wealth. I understood that all of
those earthly things were still available, but God would provide them
as I faithfully followed Christ and sought after his kingdom.

The next account in the story of Peter is found in the first two
chapters in the book of Acts. We know that from the time of Jesus's
crucifixion to the events recorded in Acts 1 was about forty-five
days. Jesus had appeared to the disciples many times during a forty-
day period following his resurrection. They met with him and he

instructed them as he had before his death. We don't know the things that were discussed during that time, but we are told of one event. It was the day when Jesus was taken up into heaven. The disciples were there and witnessed his ascension. Jesus gave them some instructions that would change their lives, the course of the church, and therefore the course of history. He instructed them to stay in Jerusalem because the promised Holy Spirit would come and baptize them there in just a few days. The disciples didn't understand this and they asked him if he meant that he would restore the kingdom to Israel at that time. Jesus replied this way: *"It is not for you to know the times or dates the Father has set by his own authority. But you will receive power when the Holy Spirit comes on you; and you will be my witnesses in Jerusalem, and in all Judea and Samaria, and to the ends of the earth"* (Acts 1:7-8).

The Holy Spirit was given on the day of Pentecost, only a few days after Jesus ascended to heaven. It happened in a simple upper room where the disciples and a few other followers of Christ were staying. The Bible says that they saw what appeared to be tongues of fire that separated and came to rest on each of them. All were filled with the Holy Spirit that day. This was a landmark day in the history of the world. Until that day, the representation of God on the earth was embodied in the person of Jesus. He was God. He performed many miracles, taught life-changing things, cast out demons, and ultimately gave his life for us as the sacrifice for our sins. But on this day, the Holy Spirit came and indwelled believers for the first time. All that Jesus had promised was now fulfilled. The new body of Christ was birthed. All followers of Christ were given the mission to complete the work of Christ on earth. They were empowered to do so by the deposit of the Holy Spirit in their spirits.

This event changed Peter's life. The restoration was done, the transformation complete. On the day of Pentecost, he stood before thousands of curious onlookers and spoke to them with such conviction and power that three thousand believed and were baptized, joining the very first church.

Restoring the Call

I saw the transformation of Peter from a well intentioned, but sometimes misguided follower of Christ to an apostle, full of the Holy Spirit and power. God's work had been completed in him. Though there were struggles that sent him reeling backward, the advent of the new Peter was completed because of the indwelling of the Holy Spirit. He had always been called. Jesus called him at the beginning as he was doing what he knew to do—fishing. Now he had fulfilled what God wanted for him. The story stopped being about him and began to be about the people he would touch. There are no more struggles mentioned in the Bible. Everything recorded about Peter from that time forward tells us of the incredible things that happened as God used him to spread the gospel, nurture the early church, and invite the rest of the world to join them.

If God could author this miraculous transformation in Peter, he could do it for me. I was experiencing many new things in my spiritual life. God had already met me, comforted me, and set me on the right pathway. But there was more. My story needed to stop being so much about me and begin to be more about Jesus and the people that he wanted me to touch. John the Baptist put it this way: *"He must increase, but I must decrease"* (John 3:30 NKJV). God was calling me to give up the things I had chosen to hold on to. He wanted me to begin to think of him more than I thought about myself. My life needed to be more about him and much less about me.

When I was seventeen years old, God called me to ministry. I knew it then as surely as I knew anything. Throughout the course of my Christian life, his calling was always part of my life. I sought to follow him anywhere he would take me. I would do whatever he asked of me. Only in the past few years had I gotten away from that calling. The restoration that was happening in my life was not necessary because I had forsaken or denied Christ, it was necessary because I had forsaken my calling. At some level, the priority of ministry decreased in my life. I didn't think about it. When it did come up, I was vague or simply refused to acknowledge that God would use me in his service. Other things became much too important.

I finally came to a place where I was able to say, "Okay God, whatever you want me to do, I will do it." In fact, not only would I be willing to do what God desired for me, I wanted it passionately. All other things became dim in the light of this new mission. Remember, I was still without a job and therefore without any income. We were literally living from day to day wondering what God would do to provide for us. But those things began to take on less importance. My life began to be more about Jesus and less about me and my needs.

I could see myself like I saw Peter. He was changed, I was changed. He had desperate moments, I had my share. He was restored, I was being restored. But one thing still lacked in me. In all of my Christian life, it seemed that I lacked the kind of Holy Spirit enabled power that Peter had. I wasn't seeing the kinds of miracles he did. I certainly wasn't seeing the kind of results he did when he preached to thousands. The same Holy Spirit that lived in him was living in me. So what needed to change?

I had to make a conscious choice to stop being self-centered in my spiritual life and begin to be Christ-centered. As I did that, things started to change. My prayers became less and less about me and began to be about others. A new love for people came. I began to pray for the saints across the world, not just those I knew. I started to uphold the church in prayer. My faith grew. I knew that significant change had happened in me. I was beginning to enter into the same source of power that Peter had. My relationship with the Holy Spirit was cultivated and began to grow. I realized that God was with me and in me all the time. If he were resident in me, then I had everything I needed to do powerful things for God. I knew that the process was ongoing, but a breakthrough had been made.

Some Words for You

I hope that the story of Peter's restoration has piqued your interest in the possibilities for your life. All of us have some failures in our lives. We have all done things we are not proud of and maybe like Peter, we were a little misguided in some of our actions. But Jesus wants to have a conversation with you. He wants to ask some personal questions about your relationship with him. Do you love him? Do you really love him? Are you absolutely sure that you love him with all of your being? These may be the very questions that God is asking of you.

Is it possible that God is using a crisis to force a confrontation with you? He certainly was in my life. I'm not sure I would have ever faced the tough questions he asked me if I had not been forced into a crisis. Peter could have run from the confrontation. I could have run from it, but we chose to answer the questions truthfully. Would you do the same? As God asks you if you love him, answer honestly. If you do love him, tell him. If you are struggling to know if you love him, tell him that. If you are angry with him, tell him. This kind of confrontation with God produces results. God is not changing. He is not moving to a new location. He is still with you just as he has always been. Your part is simply to answer him honestly.

Perhaps there is a need for you to repent. Remember, repentance is not simply confessing your sin to God. It is the deep sense of godly sorrow you feel, followed by a change of mind. Really, it is an act that is very similar to faith. Faith is belief followed by action. Repentance is sorrow followed by change. Both faith and repentance require us to act. God isn't going to do it for us. We have to make the decision ourselves. He will force the confrontation to bring us to a place where we will face the issues, but ultimately it is our decision to respond.

The fullness of the Holy Spirit is available to us just as it was on the day of Pentecost in the upper room. The Book of Acts tells us that he came and appeared as tongues of fire that lit on each person. The word picture here is one of fire. The fire of the Holy Spirit is still a vital part of the Christian life. If you have a relationship with Jesus, the flame of the Holy Spirit is in you. But our responsibility is to fan that spark into a flame that is evident to all. This happens through repentance and change. In Revelation 3:15-16, Jesus said to the church at Laodicea, *"I know your deeds, that you are neither cold nor hot. I wish that you were either one or the other! So, because you are lukewarm—neither hot nor cold—I am about to spit you out of my mouth."* These are harsh words coming from the mouth of our Lord and Savior, but this illustrates how intent he is on seeing us respond to the Holy Spirit. You and I have to make a choice. Riding the fence is worse than choosing one way or the other. I pray that you will choose to become *hot* for Christ. Stop living a mundane Christian life and fan into flame the strength that is resident in you through the Holy Spirit.

God has called you. It doesn't matter if you have felt the call to full-time ministry or not. All of us have been commissioned by God. When I talk to Christians, I am amazed at the diverse kinds of callings there are. What is the passion God has given you? What kinds of things has he asked you to do for his kingdom? It may be a desire to talk to your friends and neighbors about Jesus. Maybe you have felt the call to missionary work, or to get involved at your church in some way. I don't know what your passion is, but God does. He placed it within you. If you have given up or your priorities have changed, allow God to rekindle that desire within you to accomplish his will for your life.

I hope you have crossed a threshold. God has done amazing things in your life to help you live within your crisis. But no longer is the emphasis on simply surviving. Now the goal is victory. His intent was never to put you through a crisis simply to see if you can survive. He always uses crisis to bring growth, change, and a victorious outcome. *"Consider it pure joy, my brothers, when you face trials of many kinds, because you know that the testing of your faith develops perseverance. Perseverance must finish its work so that you may be mature and complete, not lacking anything"* (James 1:2-4). This may be one of the most difficult statements in the Bible to understand. But it is true. This is God's desire for you. Although it may be impossible to comprehend right now, you can go through your crisis and come out mature and complete. This is the goal. In other words, victory is at hand!

10
"WAIT FOR ME"

Waiting for the Lord
"Wait for the Lord, be strong and take heart and wait for the LORD."

PSALM 27:14

Waiting—there are few things in life that are as difficult to do. In the modern world we live in, we have instant access to virtually anything. In fact, we get impatient if we cannot have it now, or see it now, or experience it now. This concept is promoted by the world media, the electronics manufacturers, and retailers. We have grown accustomed to just swiping the card and walking out of the store with whatever we desire. We don't have to wait to earn the money to pay. We can simply use the credit card. These are the ways of the world we live in, but this is not the way of the Lord. He has a completely different idea about our relationship with him and how he influences and changes our lives.

I found that I had a misunderstanding of what it means to wait. I imagined that waiting involved sitting idly and killing time while I waited for what I wanted to arrive. This notion applied not only to the material things I wanted, but it also moved into my ideology; that is my understanding of spiritual things. I have always been a little impatient, and my belief in God told me that he could do it right now. I could hear what he was saying right now. I could have the necessary gifting right now. In many things this is true, but when God is doing foundation-shaking, life-changing things in a life, it often involves waiting.

In the days of my struggle, I found myself waiting all the time. Since I had no steady source of income, I was always waiting for money or other provisions to come. There was nothing I could depend on in this world. The paycheck would not be there on the first day of each month. The checkbook was not being replenished on a regular basis. So routine things I used to do—grocery shopping, purchasing items for yard maintenance, buying tools, and filling up at the gas pump—were no longer as easy as swiping the card, loading the purchased items and driving away. There were times when Cathy and I would talk and pray about what to do. Should we purchase gas for the car or buy groceries? Should we pay the bill that was due in a few days or purchase our necessities and trust God to provide? We had not had to make these kinds of decisions for many years. I was always employed, doing well, and we were taken care of. But now, we had to wait.

From the day I lost my job throughout the duration of the crisis, I found a great deal of comfort by reading the book of Psalms. I could not find that comfort within myself. Many people brought comforting words to me, but somehow it didn't calm me. But when I read the Psalms, I found that the words written there were like a deep peace in the tumultuous storm within my soul. David's psalms seemed to express exactly what I could not. The words written there led me into many deep truths that changed me from the inside out.

One of those scriptures was Psalm 27:14 referenced above. This verse changed the way I viewed the idea of waiting. As I thought about it, I realized that waiting is not a passive activity. In fact, it is one of the most aggressive ways to seek God. I began to understand that as I was waiting for God, he was doing some pretty spectacular things in me. These were things that only he could do. And he could only accomplish those things while I was waiting.

One of my earliest childhood memories took place when I was three or four years old. Several months before Christmas, my mother took me shopping. We went to a nearby town and visited many stores. My job was to simply keep up with my mom! She did everything in high gear. Most of my memory of that trip is simply hanging on to her hand and being, at times, nearly drug to the next store. But there was one significant thing I remembered. Her plan that day was to look over the toy sections and make a list of things she thought my siblings and I would like to have for Christmas. Looking back, I know my parents did not have a lot of money, but they were thoughtful and always managed to provide wonderful holiday times for our family.

One store had a large toy section. Of course, I was looking up at most everything on the shelves, and we sped by most of the toys so fast that I didn't have time to take it all in. But we stopped by one shelf and I saw the best toy (in my mind) ever made. It was, and I am dating myself here, a pull-string, talking Bugs Bunny. I'm not talking about the kind of electronic talking toy that is common today. This toy required you to pull the string and as it recoiled back to its original position, the Bugs would talk. He said his most famous lines like; "What's up, Doc!" and many more. It kind of sounded like an old vinyl record inside, but that was perfectly fine with me. He was big— maybe half my size, and he left an unforgettable impression on me.

I knew my mom saw how much I loved that toy. But she underestimated my memory and the impression the toy left on me. I have talked to her about this incident and she remembers it well. She honestly thought that I would not remember seeing the toy. She would buy it and give it to me on Christmas day. But I did remember. In fact, I was absolutely positive that I would get the Bugs for Christmas. But I had to wait. I don't know how long it was, but it seemed like a long time to a three-year-old. I'm sure I thought about it every day. I was excited in anticipation of receiving the gift. Christmas came and there was a large gift under the tree with my name on it. I don't remember anything else I received that Christmas. But I got what I was waiting for.

I learned that waiting for God is a lot like that experience. There is excitement, anticipation, and hope. There are also times of doubt, concern, and anxiety. It is not easy to wait for God. He had done some amazing things in my life. As you have read, there were many foundations already laid in my spirit. Yet through all of this, there was still a deep understanding that I was waiting. I was waiting for my crisis to end. I knew there was much more for me on the other side of this experience. But getting from where I was to where I would be, involved . . . waiting.

Psalm 27:14 gives some very specific instructions in regard to waiting for God. These things seemed distant. They seemed too ambiguous for me to grasp. But I continued to meditate on that scripture. As I did, I gained insight into the instructions.

Be strong. This is the first instruction. As I searched to understand what this meant to me, I realized that this was a process that was already taking place inside me. When I was secure in my job, my finances and my routine, there was a certain amount of spiritual weakness. I was depending on those things as my source of strength rather than God. It was easy to think that I was in a strong position because of my secure circumstances. However, I learned that these things are not secure at all. In fact, they can and do change in an instant. They are consumed like paper in a fire. What was now being accomplished in my life, however, was strong. These were things that God was placing in me to make me spiritually strong. Things like repentance, faith, putting on the armor, fellowshipping with him, and learning about his kingdom were developing in me a spiritual strength that I had never experienced in my life. Instead of allowing my circumstance to dictate how I lived, I began to live according to God's promises and instruction. This, my friends, was strength. So without even knowing, I was obeying the first instruction found there. This was not a strength that I could find within myself, it was being deposited in me by the Holy Spirit. And I began to pray, "God, give me more strength to wait for you."

Take heart. How could I do that? People all over the world are given that instruction at one time or another in their lives. Usually, this is the idea that you have to "buck up," or "find courage" within yourself. But I knew that there was no courage in me. I did not have the strength of character within myself to obey this instruction. Then I discovered that the answer didn't really lie inside of me at all. It was found in my trust in God. I had to ask myself: Do I trust him? Do I believe that he wants the best for me? Do I really believe that he will deliver me from times of trouble? With all of the things God had shown me and built in me, the answer to all of these questions was yes, I really did trust him. So I did not have to find the courage or strength of character within myself. I took heart in the fact that he is God and I trusted him completely.

I found that the first things necessary for me while waiting for God was to rely on the strength that he had already placed in me. When I did that, I was able to take heart in the fact that I trusted him completely. Throughout the entire process, he had never let me down or failed me. I knew I could count on him. If he said that I should wait, I would do that with all my heart.

Waiting was difficult for another reason. There was always pressure from family, friends, and well-meaning Christians to do something about the situation. They equated strength and character of heart with action. The pressure was always there for me to go out and make something happen. However, if God had said, "Wait for me," it was critical that I did just that. There was often criticism for waiting. But I believed what God had said. I wanted the best he had for my life and I had learned by then to obey what he said.

Let me share three more things I learned about waiting for God. These things are vitally important when God tells us to wait:

1. WAIT IN EXPECTATION.

*"In the morning, O LORD, you hear my voice; in the morning
I lay my requests before you and wait in expectation."*

PSALM 5:3

What good is waiting if you are not expecting something? When I was waiting for Christmas to come to receive my Bugs Bunny, I was expecting something. This is what gave me the strength and patience to get through. This is especially true when we are waiting for God. Are we to sit and wait for him to show up? No! The psalmist said that he laid his requests before the Lord every morning.

I continued to pray and seek God every day. For me, waiting was not an idle activity; it was full of the expectation that God was going to hear my prayers and accomplish what I asked him to do. This gets back to the root of faith. Faith is believing and expecting him to do what we ask. I understood that. My waiting time became a time of joyfully expecting a God-sized answer to my prayers.

2. WAIT IN HOPE.

*"We wait in hope for the LORD;
he is our help and our shield."*

PSALM 33:20

Faith and hope go together. Faith is defined by our belief and our actions. Hope is defined as a belief in a positive outcome related to events and circumstances in one's life. Hope is the feeling that what is wanted can be had or that events will turn out for the best. It is not necessarily a physical emotion, but rather a spiritual understanding. It is not positive thinking. It is a deep-seated, spiritual knowledge that a positive outcome is guaranteed. Hope is in some ways easier to grasp than faith. We have learned throughout our lives to hope for things. But hope in the life of a Christian takes on a new dimension. When you insert hope into waiting for God, there is an energetic and positive belief that it is not in vain, but rather a necessary decision to allow God to accomplish all he desires in us. When we take this approach, waiting becomes not only tolerable, but also enjoyable.

I discovered that adding hope to my waiting experience made it much easier to deal with and to understand. I was not just waiting for God to show up and rescue me from my situation. I was expecting something even better. Hope was something I could grasp. I hoped for the promises I read in the Bible. I hoped for all the secrets of the kingdom to be revealed and the bounty of the kingdom to be released into my life. I began to focus on the outcome and not the waiting time. It was as if what I was hoping for had already happened, all I had to do was see it become a reality.

3. BE STILL AND WAIT.

"Be still before the LORD and wait patiently for him."

PSALM 37:7

This may be the most difficult task associated with waiting. In times of prayer, it is difficult to simply be quiet and allow God to speak. It seems easier for us to speak rather than to listen. But when we are waiting for the Lord, we must learn to be still. This does not mean that we shouldn't bring our needs before him. We should, and we should do that with full faith. But we want to see things happen. We want to make things happen. The purpose in waiting is to allow God to bring the answer in his time and in his way. When we do that, we are guaranteed the best result. God is absolutely in love with us and he wants the very best for us. If we circumvent the process and take matters into our own hands, we will end up with a less than desirable result.

The psalmist tells us that we must be still and be patient. I know that in the middle of my circumstance, it was not easy to do either. I have a difficult time being still for anything, and I have already confessed to you that I have always struggled with impatience. I believe the purpose for my waiting period was not just for the result that I wanted, but for the result that God wanted. His desire was for me to overcome my impatience and learn to relax. I was not waiting just for the blessing he would bring. He was using that time to create patience in me.

God Waits

> *"Jesus loved Martha and her sister and Lazarus.*
> *Yet when he heard that Lazarus was sick,*
> *he stayed where he was two more days."*
> John 11:5-6

I have focused on our need to wait for God. However, it is very important for us to understand that God waits as well. He knows our needs, he knows exactly when and how to bring the answer or the deliverance. Often, this is not in the time frame we desire. To us, it seems that he is always late. In reality, he comes at the perfect time to touch and bless us and to bring glory to himself.

There is a story found in John 11 about Jesus and his relationship to two sisters and a brother. Their names were Mary, Martha, and Lazarus. Although we do not know a lot about the background, we do know that Jesus was very close to this family, particularly Lazarus. They had become friends, but Jesus's ministry took him away to other communities and away from their friendship.

The two sisters sent word to Jesus informing him that Lazarus was sick. When they sent word, they referred to Lazarus as "the one you love." Their hope was that Jesus would come immediately and heal their brother. They knew Jesus and had full confidence that he could and would do this. However, when Jesus received the message, he did not come but instead chose to stay where he was for two more days. In that time, Lazarus died.

By the time Jesus arrived in Bethany, where the family lived, the body of Lazarus had already been prepared and placed in a tomb. He had been there for four days. The sisters were distraught and told him that if he had only been there, their brother would not have died. Yet Jesus had a greater plan than they could imagine. The Lord asked Martha if she believed he was the Christ. She did believe in him and in his ability to do anything. So they made their way to the place where Lazarus was entombed.

Jesus was moved by his love for Lazarus. We are told that *"Jesus wept"* when he was at the tomb of his friend. Then he looked up to heaven and thanked his Father for always hearing him. He said this was to show the glory of God to those who had gathered there.

Finally, Jesus spoke in a loud voice and commanded Lazarus to come forth from the tomb. Immediately he walked out of the cave with his grave clothes still on him. Jesus instructed those there to take the grave clothes off of him and let him go. It was done. Lazarus had been raised from the dead after four days.

This story illustrates to us several things about the character of Jesus. First, we need to understand that sometimes God waits. He doesn't always come exactly when we think he should. When we think the situation can't get any worse or that we can't survive any longer, God still waits because he has a plan that far surpasses what we see. Next, we have to know how very much Jesus loves us. In fact, he loves us enough to allow us to go through difficult times and still wait to bring our deliverance. Jesus wept over Lazarus. He weeps over us as well. We must never allow ourselves to think that God is angry and enjoys seeing us suffer. In fact, it is exactly the opposite. He goes through the crisis with us. He comforts us, teaches us, and encourages us. Then at just the right time, our answer comes.

God does all things to display his glory to the world. Jesus didn't get to Lazarus in time to keep him from dying. Yet he chose to wait so the incredible miracle could be witnessed by many people. Glory was given to God, and Jesus was proven once again to be the chosen Son of God. It is the same in our time of testing. God sometimes waits, but while we are waiting for him, his glory is being displayed for all to see.

Some Words for You

In my time of crisis, God wanted me to wait. Is he asking you to wait for him? If he gives you clear direction and a plan then by all means obey him. But if there doesn't seem to be a way out, if there is no direction from him, wait. While you are waiting, don't sit idly by, passively waiting for something different to happen. Seek him with all your heart. Allow him to reach deep within you and build you up until you are literally a new person.

Be strong and take heart. Find this in Jesus. He is your source of strength. Do you trust him? Do you believe that he loves you and wants the absolute best for you? Ask yourself these questions. If your strength is found in the work he does in your life, and if your heart is to trust him with your whole life, wait for him. If you are struggling with your willingness to trust him, ask him to show you how he cares for you. He wants to help you through your difficult time and deliver you from it with amazing results.

Expect God to do something great. Hope for the day when you are free. But most of all, quiet yourself and be still before the Lord. When you do that, you will find that he loves to talk to you. He loves to have a conversation that involves both of you. Too many times, we do all the talking and he simply waits for us to finish so he can speak. It is vital to "*be still and know that he is God.*"

Finally, understand that God is using your crisis to bring glory to himself. Do you know that other people are watching? They are waiting to see what will happen in your life. If you will surrender to God and his timing, if you will wait for him, he will be glorified, all the world will see how much he loves you, and they will see his deliverance in your life. So will you!

11

"I USE BROKEN VESSELS"

Learning to Speak His Word

"Now, Lord, consider their threats and enable your servants
to speak your word with great boldness."

ACTS 4:29

The Word of God became vitally important to me during the days of my crisis. I had read the Bible for many years, but I had never really understood the incredible importance of its impact on my life. It is very difficult to articulate the kind of change that occurred in me regarding the Word of God. Before, I understood the importance of his written Word, but I found that I would only receive the things that seemed to suit me. I would say that I believed it, but in reality, I was only willing to accept the parts that helped me at the time. But now, in the middle of a difficult circumstance, God was giving me a new outlook on his Word. If I said that I believed God's Word, I would have to be willing to accept it all, not just the appealing parts. I found that it could speak amazing encouragement to me and it could speak things that humbled me, disciplined me, and corrected me.

The definitive narrative on the Word of God is found in Psalm 119. There is a wealth of knowledge there about reading, meditating, applying, and living the Word. I love verse 160: *"The entirety of Your*

word is truth, and every one of Your righteous judgments endures forever"
(NKJV). I learned that when I read God's Word, I am seeing a perfect
reflection of God's character. This gave me a new understanding of
the truths written there. No longer were they simply rules to follow
or nice stories that didn't really apply to me. I was actually getting
glimpses of God himself through reading those words.

Everything that God said to me was already written in his Word.
He would take a Bible verse and bring it to life for me. I may have
read that scripture many times, but the Holy Spirit would use it at just
the right time to bring a new insight or answer to me. I have written
many very personal things in the preceding pages. These were things
that I believe were spoken to me directly by God himself. And every
one of those things was based on and founded in the written Word
of God. I learned that this is how God speaks. His Word has already
been established in heaven. So he recorded those words so that I could
apply them, and therefore, it would be established on earth in my life.

As I wrote earlier, God had shown me the importance of speaking
his Word. I had learned that God created everything by the spoken
word and he had placed that same ability in us. When we speak,
something is created. It may not always be good, but something is
brought into existence through our words. So it became a regular
part of my daily life to speak the Word of God. Each time I did this,
I became bolder. I would declare it to the heavens, and soon I was
speaking the Word to friends and family. I learned that my speech
was being seasoned with the salt of the Word as I spoke to people.

A great breakthrough took place when I began to speak the Word
and pray prophetically. I noticed that my prayers changed. When I
would confess sin before God, instead of asking him to cleanse me
from unrighteousness, I would proclaim it as already done. "Lord,
thank you that you have already forgiven me and cleansed me from
all unrighteousness. I have confessed my sin and you have already
cleansed me!" I also began speaking prophetic things over my life

and others. I would declare in the face of unemployment and lack of income, "These are the days of increase and abundance. This is the season of the favor of the Lord!" I experienced a new kind of power. This was really bringing the kingdom of God to my life and the lives of others. I knew God had already established these things in heaven. So I was simply speaking what had already occurred.

When I became willing to receive God's Word in its entirety, it led me to some things that were unexpected. The rebuilding process that God was undertaking in my life was far from complete. I still needed to deal with some old issues, accept some difficult direction, and receive God's work of bringing about character change.

Learning Humility

"Blessed are the poor in spirit,
for theirs is the kingdom of heaven."
"Blessed are the meek, for they will inherit the earth."
Matthew 5:3, 5

Humility is a key of the kingdom of heaven. In my experience with the Lord, I have found that I must be humble. The process of being humbled can be easy or it can be difficult. Either I could choose to humble myself before God, or he could humble me. The crisis of losing my job and career was certainly humbling. I believe God had a purpose for allowing that to happen. That purpose was to help me to stop being self-reliant, become humble, and trust him with my entire life. So my crisis was being used by God to perfect my character.

I enjoy the game of football and have already shared with you in a previous chapter a life lesson I learned through playing. A close friend related a story from his playing days that helped to teach him humility.

He was a young player at the time and rarely saw playing time in games. But one particular week, he had done so well in practice that the coach asked him if he would take the honor of leading the team onto the field before that week's game. Of course he was very excited and thought about it constantly on the day of the game.

Game time came and the team left the locker room with my friend leading the way. He was so excited and proud at what he was doing that all sense of those around him, coaches and players, seemed distant. The team was to run through a large paper poster that had been made by the students of the school. It was being held by the cheerleading squad. Of course all the spectators were already gathered, cheering the team as they walked to the edge of the field.

The coach gave the word and the time had come for him to run through that giant poster with the rest of his teammates following. The adrenalin rushed through him as he ran full speed with his arms uplifted in exuberance. He ran through the poster, dashed in front of the crowd all the way to the other end of the field. He was overwhelmed with excitement until . . . he turned around and saw that none of the other team members or coaches were with him. In his excitement, he had blocked out everything else but the pride he felt in the moment. He had run to the wrong end of the field. When he looked, he saw the team gathered at the other end. The one hundred-yard jog in front of a laughing crowd seemed like it took an eternity.

He learned something about humility that day. He learned that he could take a humble approach to anything, any honor or recognition, or he could be prideful. He thought that everyone would surely praise him because of this great event. Instead, he was embarrassed and felt the shame of creating a laughable spectacle.

I realized that any honor that I had received from my position in employment was gone. I thought I was indispensible. I was the manager. The company could not be run as effectively with anyone else. I found that none of these things were true. I was quickly and startlingly released. There was no glory and no honor.

God used my crisis to teach me about humility. I would never say that God caused me to be fired from my job. I would say that he used the circumstance to teach me a valuable lesson. Now it was my turn to understand that and make a choice to be humble before the Lord. Jesus said, *"For whoever exalts himself will be humbled, and he who humbles himself will be exalted* (Luke 14:11 NKJV). This is the truth of the kingdom. I was at a point in my life when I wanted everything God had to give me. I wanted the completeness of his kingdom in me. So I wanted to learn to use the key of humility.

God's kingdom seems to work completely opposite to the way our world works. Here, we exalt people who are wealthy or powerful. People esteem them and desire to be like they are. We read books that tell us how the rich man got that way or the powerful man rose to that pinnacle. However, God declares that his kingdom belongs to those who are like little children, those who are weak. He says we should be poor in spirit and meek. He boldly tells us that the least will be the greatest in his kingdom.

I focused on the blessings Jesus pronounced in Matthew 5. We call these the beatitudes. In other words, we are to exercise the character qualities listed there to receive the blessings he pronounced. I learned that I needed literally to be like these people in order to really enter into his kingdom.

To be *poor in spirit* means to be 'humble'. It is an understanding that within myself, I am nothing. I have nothing that has not been given to me by God himself. These are humbling thoughts. My talents, abilities and my successes have all been given to me. They are not a result of my own greatness. I learned that this didn't disallow me from speaking or using my talents. In fact, it freed me to do just that. When I began to give honor to God and take none for myself, it meant that it was his reputation, not mine that was on the line. If I were really humble, God would be glorified and exalted. It is only through the practice of being humble that I would receive the totality of the kingdom in my everyday life.

I asked God to make me a meek person. This was a difficult prayer for me because I had always equated meekness with weakness.

I thought meek people were the ones who were afraid to do anything. They would never confront an issue or deal with a disagreement. But God has a different view of meekness. He esteems the meek as great and powerful people. I have heard it said that *meekness* is 'power under control.' I believe this is true. Meek people are willing to accept the fact that everything they have is given to them by God. They are content with the results. They are not weaklings. Instead, they exercise the ultimate form of strength and power by relying completely on God.

This is the kind of life God wanted me to lead. The more I thought about it and prayed, the more peace I felt at the prospect of completely relying on him. To be meek and humble meant that I would have to abandon all my self-reliance and pride. I would have to realize that my strength is in Christ alone.

When I actually began to live as a meek and humble person, things changed. I esteemed others greater than myself. As I did that, I began to experience new love for them. This included my family and friends. All the things that irritated me about their personalities began to be much less important. I was viewing them as God does. They are people he created, just as he created me. They are people he died for, just as he died for me. I had never considered myself to be a judgmental person. But I experienced a new freedom to simply love people instead of fighting through my own tainted opinions of them.

The total picture of what God was doing in my life was now coming together. Until this point, it seemed like he was randomly changing different areas of my soul. But after nearly two months, he had exposed many different areas that needed to be changed in me, and he had provided the revelation to accomplish it. When I looked at the broad picture, I saw that he was bringing me back to the fundamentals of my relationship with him. He had challenged me to experience new faith, humility, healing, and restoration. But he wasn't finished yet. There were still lessons to be learned while I dealt with my crisis.

LEARNING PERSEVERANCE

> *"Blessed is the man who perseveres under trial,*
> *because when he has stood the test, he will receive the crown*
> *of life that God has promised those who love him."*
>
> JAMES 1:12

> *"We also glory in tribulations, knowing that*
> *tribulation produces perseverance; and perseverance,*
> *character; and character, hope."*
>
> ROMANS 5:3-4 NKJV

There is nothing easy about trials and tribulation. These times are very difficult for us to contend with. But from God's perspective, these are times when he can mold us into the people he created us to be. I learned during my struggle that I could grow in my relationship with God dramatically as I sought after him. As difficult as it is to understand, God uses these times to perfect our character. He knew that I was ready to learn some valuable lessons in my walk with him. He had comforted me in my great need, he had challenged me in areas of my faith, and now he wanted to work on my character.

The scriptures above pointed out some vital things that I needed to learn. The first and possibly most difficult was perseverance. I would have much preferred for God to rescue me from my crisis and move me to the next season of my life. But the reality was: God wanted me to learn perseverance through the difficult time. There would be no early escape. I could not remove myself from the situation. Only God could do that and his timing had not yet come. In fact, I would have to endure my trial for much more time than I desired.

To *persevere* means 'to persist in a state, enterprise or undertaking in spite of counterinfluence, opposition or discouragement' (Webster's Dictionary). This definition certainly illustrates the difficulty of accomplishing such a task. God wanted me to learn to persist even in the face of obvious discouragement. Perseverance always requires time. What would perseverance be if the circumstance were over quickly? As little as I relished the thought, it was going to take time for my crisis to end. But the promises associated with learning to persevere far outweigh the discomfort of continuing in the struggle.

If perseverance were necessary only to learn how to persist in the circumstance, that would have been valuable in itself. But God did not stop with that. You see, perseverance produces other results. I could not have learned greater things, or experienced the changes in my life, or grown in my relationship with Jesus had I not first learned to persevere in the trial. The reality is this: my character was in need of more change and I needed to learn how to hope again. The key to these things was found in perseverance.

The change that needed to continue in me was in regard to my character. Have you ever heard the phrase, "a person of character?" That statement usually refers to a person who is full of integrity, can be trusted implicitly, and is always honest. I longed to be that kind of person. Romans 8:29 (NKJV) tells us; *"For whom he foreknew, He also predestined to be conformed to the image of His Son, that He might be the firstborn among many brethren."* This is the ultimate picture of a person of character. This was what God was calling me to be. He did not want me to conform to the world or to my own ideas of what greatness would look like. I was to be conformed to the image of Jesus. What he looked like is how I am to look. How he spoke is how I am to speak. How he lived is how I am to live. There was no escaping this. God wanted me to conform to his image. And perseverance led me to that place.

Perseverance leads to character and character produces hope. What hope did I need to experience? First, I needed to know the hope that I would be delivered from my trial. That was the most urgent hope necessary. Without this hope, I would fail the test of the trial and not complete what God had in store for me. He had already told me in several ways that his intent was to deliver me from this circumstance. He would make the way of escape for me. Secondly, I needed to grasp the hope that there is a "crown of life" waiting for me. After all, as a Christian, this is the ultimate goal. But I have learned that this crown can be available to me right now as I experience the kingdom of heaven in my life here on earth. With this in mind, the hope is attainable. There came an excitement when I realized that these promises from God are not only for the next life, but also are available to me in this one. He wants me to experience heaven now. He wants to show me the glory of his presence.

So perseverance, however challenging, was the pathway to experiencing this change of character and new hope that is only found in my relationship with God. Once I realized the importance of these things, it allowed me to continue through the circumstance with purpose. I knew that God was accomplishing great things in me. So I experienced a new resolve to persevere and reap the benefits that came as a result.

MENDING BROKEN RELATIONSHIPS
"And when you stand praying, if you hold anything against anyone, forgive him, so that your Father in heaven may forgive you your sins."
MARK 11:25

I have a friend who is the pastor of a large church in a neighboring state. I had not seen him for several years. In fact, we had not been in contact for much of that time. He was invited by my pastor to come to our church and speak. We made arrangements to have lunch together and catch up on each other's lives. In the course of his visit, he shared some things the Lord had given him to teach. One of those things was the importance of reconciling relationships that had been damaged or even lost. He talked about the fact that we don't know how long we have to be here on earth. The worst possible thing would be to run out of time having not mended the separation of ruined relationships.

As he said these things, I realized that I had some broken relationships that had occurred in my life. In some cases, I could remember a confrontation that caused the rift. Other relationships just seemed to be lost over the course of time and distance. But I began to realize that there is no room in the kingdom of heaven for people who are separated from one another because of a silly argument or lack of attentiveness. So I heard the instruction from the Lord to begin to face these relationships head-on.

The stark realization that broken relationships hinders my connection with God gave me the desire to take care of some of these relationships. I found the problem in some cases was not that I held something against the other person, but rather that that person held something against me. So what could I do about that? Was it my responsibility to contact those people and clear the air with them? For the answers to these questions, I asked the One who knew about all of those relationships—God.

I discovered the answers lie in part in the scripture referenced above. If my prayers were hindered, in other words, if God reminded me of a broken relationship while I was praying, I had a responsibility to respond to his prompting and act. That action depended on what God asked me to do. I began to lay these relationships before him. I also examined myself. If I held any ill will against a person, it was my responsibility to repent, change my attitude, and receive forgiveness from the person and from God. If the other person held something against me, I needed to seek God and ask him to guide me in the next steps toward mending the relationship.

I found that there were a few broken relationships with which I did hold something against the other person. Some of these relationships dealt with people who were, in part, responsible for my dismissal from my job. In these cases, these people were not Christians. They were not the kind of friendships like I had with other brothers and sisters. These were professional relationships. Everything about them was associated with our place of employment. So my responsibility was simply to give my anger, hurt, and frustration to God. I had to dismiss the destructive thoughts I had toward these people. These thoughts had no spiritual value. In fact, they hindered my relationship with God. So I made decisions to give these old relationships to him and receive cleansing. When a hurtful or vengeful thought came to me, I took it captive and made it obedient to Christ. Soon, those thoughts stopped coming. These relationships were over. The other people had gone their way and I had gone mine. There was nothing to mend. But there was healing for me as I yielded them to God. I actually began to pray for those people. I asked God to bring them to a place where they would realize their great need and give their lives to him.

There were also damaged relationships with other Christians. If God reminded me of a specific relationship, I would ask him what to do. In some cases, it involved me contacting them. In other cases, the Lord created divine appointments for me with that person.

One "appointment" was with a friend who had been very close to me in the past. He was a fellow worker in ministry and had stood with me through good times and bad. Although there was no confrontation that separated us, there was a circumstance that required both of us to take a stand. His stand differed from mine. Although we did not argue or intentionally back away from each other, there was a barrier. This circumstance had happened many years ago, and over the course of time, both of us were removed geographically from the place of the issue. The relationships we had both developed with others there were intact, but we had all moved on to the next seasons of our lives.

Although he lived in another state, we were brought together by a mutual friend. We were both invited to a gathering of old friends. Many of the people there I had not seen for fifteen to twenty years. As all of us met and spent time together, it was as if no time had passed at all. We reminisced and laughed as we recalled old times that we spent together. There came a moment when my friend and I were left alone. I remember looking him in the eye and through tears, simply saying, "I've missed you!" He responded by pulling me into a heartfelt embrace. Although nothing was mentioned about the old issue, there was healing that took place in me that day.

I learned that relationships with other Christians are so important that I could not allow separations that I had caused to remain. God was exposing them, and my part was simply to respond to him in the way he directed me. In this way, my prayers would go unhindered and others would be released from the bondage that broken relationships carry.

These days were difficult times in my crisis. Although I was more emotionally prepared to deal with the new things God was doing, these were tough things. The realization that my circumstance was not over but was being used by God to change me was both comforting and challenging. More than anything, I wanted to move into a new era in my life. But these things I learned: the importance of the Word, the blessing of humility, the call to persevere, and the need to mend relationships would be some of the most important lessons I would ever receive.

Some Words for You

God's Word is vitally important to us. As you grow in your relationship with him, you will find that his Word becomes more and more critical to your life. I want to encourage you in a new way to view the Word. Begin to see it as wholly and completely true. View every word as being uttered from the mouth of God directly to you. When you do this, you will find that your desire to read his Word will increase exponentially. You will begin to think about the Word. As this takes place, you cannot help but speak it. When you grasp this truth, you will begin to prophesy over your own life. His Word is truth in every word written. You can depend on it. Apply it to your life, receive new revelation from him and move into greater relationship with the Creator of the Universe.

I cannot emphasize enough how important humility is to us as believers. It is much easier to humble yourself than it is to be humbled by God. Learn to live a life of humility. When you esteem others greater than yourself, you will build vital new relationships. These people can and will be used by God to strengthen and encourage you. And you, in turn, will bless them. Humility is an important key in the kingdom of God. Without it, you cannot experience all that God is offering. You must become like a little child. You must claim to know nothing but Christ and him crucified. You must abandon the draw of the world to believe that riches and power are the ultimate success. You must become the least and God will make you the greatest.

I pray that you will persevere through your crisis. You have come so far, do not abandon the great things God is accomplishing in you. Although it is a tough pill to swallow, it may take time for you to escape your trial and enter into the new season of life God has prepared for you. Don't despair! Your perseverance will lead to new character and new hope being established in you. These things will carry you through the balance of your circumstance. Do this and the crown of life awaits!

If you have relationships that are broken, allow God to give you direction toward repairing the breech. I encourage you to take the approach I did. If you feel your prayers are being hindered because of broken or damaged relationships, ask God what to do. He will tell you. People often talk about the "elephant in the room." This is when there is a huge issue that no one will talk about. Well, God exposes the elephant! He wants you to deal with it so it will not hinder you in any way. God will never allow us to harbor ill feelings toward others. He will always talk about it and expose it. Your part is simply to respond and do what he tells you to do.

Take heart! Your crisis will fade into the next season of your life. But while you are here, glean every spiritual benefit you can! Open yourself up to the Father and allow him to establish his kingdom in you. Like me, you will be able to say, "It was the most difficult time of my life, but it was the best time with God I've ever experienced." As you move into next big thing he has, you will never forget the deep things he accomplished during this time. You will not forget and God will build on what you have learned.

12

"I HAVE A PURPOSE FOR YOU"

Rising from Defeat

"But thanks be to God! He gives us the victory through our Lord Jesus Christ."

1 CORINTHIANS 15:57

I discovered that often I would wake up in the morning with a word or phrase in my mind and on my lips. It is interesting how the Holy Spirit does that. Often, these things were simply there. I didn't remember dreaming anything that would lead to these morning blessings. But I came to realize that this was one of the ways that God chose to speak to me. In every case, these words turned out to be very important to my life. The words always spoke to where I was in my life at that particular time, or to the circumstance at that moment or where he intended to lead me in the future.

One of those phrases came one morning near the end of my sixty days. The phrase is: *"Out of what seems to be your greatest defeat will come your greatest victory."* This was a life-changing concept for me! Until that moment, I still had the mentality that my crisis would end by God delivering me from it. I believed that it would be a miraculous release from the prison of my circumstance. Although I continue to believe God was doing just that, his plan was for more than just to rescue me. He was telling me that he would use what appeared to be a great defeat and turn it around to be a great victory in my life and the future he had for me.

This led me to view and understand my crisis time in a completely different light. I knew God would rescue me from it. I would enter into a new season in my life and my relationship with him. But in the middle of my crisis, it was difficult to see how I could actually be a victor. Each day had challenges that seemed insurmountable. But God answered me in my need and helped me get through the struggle. That had been the pattern. But a new revelation from him was changing all that. If his plan was to use my circumstance to bring the greatest victory I would ever experience, I needed to believe it and participate in it.

As I thought about what it meant to gain the greatest victory out of defeat, I was reminded of two of the greatest examples that could be imagined. Both of these were men who were prominent in the stories and writing of the New Testament. I knew the stories of their defeats and victories well. The victories that came through these two men far exceeded anything I might experience. I had yet to see the victory the Lord was speaking about, but I knew the defeat. I was still living there. So the stories of these men gave me great hope about the possibilities of what God had in store for me.

The first example is Jesus. He experienced many victories in his ministry on the earth. He saw miracles beyond anything that had ever been seen. The blind saw, the deaf heard, the lame walked, and those oppressed by the enemy were set free. Yet in the last days of his life, the apparent defeat came. Because Jesus was the Son of God, he knew that this defeat was not permanent. But to those who were his closest friends and followers, this looked like the ultimate defeat.

The Master and Teacher they had come to love and follow was taken captive, tortured beyond comprehension, and sentenced to die the agonizing death of crucifixion. That sentence was carried out and in two short days from the time of his arrest, the King of kings was dead. I imagine the loss those followers felt. They became quite literally, "sheep without a shepherd." Many of them had left everything, including their families, to follow the Messiah. And now he was gone. It must have seemed that all was lost and they had wasted years of their lives.

Meanwhile, Satan was squealing with glee. His ultimate plan had been accomplished. He had tempted Jesus three years earlier. He offered him all the kingdoms of the world. He offered power, wealth, and fame. But Jesus had declined and rebuked him to his face. So the plan he had hatched to defeat Jesus had now been completed. Judas had done his job by handing Jesus over to the Pharisees. The Pharisees had done their job by accusing and manipulating his words and actions. Everything was completed and finally, Jesus was dead. Satan thought he had won. It was all over.

But, out of what looked like the greatest defeat in the history of mankind, victory emerged. Jesus rose from the grave. Death no longer had mastery over him. He had defeated death and taken the keys away from Satan. He became the sacrificial Lamb for all mankind. No longer would any person be denied access to heaven. He paid a debt, a great debt, and he did it once and for all! What great victory rose from the darkest defeat! This one sacrificial act changed the world forever.

The second story from the Bible is the account of the apostle Paul. Like Jesus, he had experienced incredible victories during his ministry. He had done many miracles, including raising a young man from the dead. He had propagated the gospel in most of the known world. Thousands had come to believe in Christ and experience the new life that Paul was preaching. Things were good. Victories had been won.

But there was a dark time that occurred in Paul's life. He too was forced to face the opposition of the Pharisees. He was forced to face trial in front of several Roman leaders. Much of the latter years of his life were spent in chains. He was a prisoner and he was shackled to a Roman guard at all times.

Again, Satan must have been jumping up and down. He had lost the battle with Jesus and much of his kingdom was stripped away. But this was redemption. This Paul was a thorn in his side. He had taken the good news of Christ to the entire Gentile world. Now there were untold numbers of Christians. Paul had been used mightily by God. The worst part for Satan to swallow was the fact that Paul had been his greatest ally in the beginning. He had persecuted the newly formed church to the point that many had been killed and put in prison. But somehow, God had taken his pawn away and used him to further his kingdom.

But now, Satan thought he had won a major victory. This man was now in chains. He would no longer be travelling the world to bring more people to the knowledge of the Messiah. He had Paul right where he wanted him—in prison. He must have been upset that he could not kill him. Jesus had taken away those keys. But the next alternative was just as effective. He was bound in chains.

Once again, a great defeat was turned into a world-changing victory. You see, Paul's ministry did not end simply because he was put in chains and imprisoned. In fact, it grew stronger. Paul began to write letters to all of the churches he had established. He encouraged them, instructed them, and led them into deeper relationships with Jesus. These letters would later become a cherished volume of scriptures referred to as the Pauline Epistles. Untold millions of Christians have been encouraged and instructed in the faith through these letters. This was not defeat, it was phenomenal victory!

Could God be telling me that I could experience the same kind of victories these men did? That was exactly what he was saying. I understood and even though I was yet to see this victory, I had a promise and validation based in what I saw in the Word. I made a decision to no longer see my crisis as a defeat. I had lived in that mentality long enough. Now I was going to look forward to and hope for the victory that God had in store for me. My greatest desire was to be used by him. I wanted to share the love of Jesus with people. I wanted to encourage the church and teach them the things I had learned from the Lord during my trial. So a new anticipation rose in me. It was the desire and the unwavering hope that my crisis would end and I would move into the real victory that God had planned. I had direction and I had passion.

EYES ON THE FUTURE

> *"From now on I will tell you of new things,*
> *of hidden things unknown to you."*
>
> ISAIAH 48:6B

In chapter 6, I shared with you some of the things the Lord told me in regard to the future. I knew he had plans for me, he told me that. I knew he did not plan to harm me. I was assured of that. But the specifics of what he wanted me to accomplish seemed distant. I wasn't sure of the future. I was at peace about it, but I did not know where it would lead me.

One day I found myself reading Isaiah 48 and 49. It was at that moment that some very important truths were revealed to me. These were things that I thought I knew about my own life, but I had never really entered into what God had intended for me. The verse I referenced above caught my attention. It was a turning point in my circumstance. God had been so faithful to comfort me when I was grieving, to draw me close to him through his instruction and to speak to me about changing my life in favor of serving him. Now it seemed as if he were saying, *"Enough about this circumstance! I am now going to speak to you about your future. I want to lead you into and through the plan I have for you."*

I love hearing the voice of God in my spirit. I have learned that he speaks to me in my mind. I have never personally heard an audible voice. But when he speaks to me, I know it. The words come so quickly that there is absolutely no way I could have thought of it on my own. It is as if he overrides my thinking and places his words of direction, encouragement, and correction there. This was one of those times. The words of that scripture jumped off the page and into my spirit. I knew that this was God speaking directly to me. He was ready to tell me about my future. These were encouraging words that said; *"You are ready for new things, hidden things are going to be revealed."*

As I read on that day, the Holy Spirit spoke to me through the prophet Isaiah:

> *Before I was born the Lord called me;*
> *from my birth He has made mention of my name.*
> *He made my mouth like a sharpened sword,*
> *in the shadow of his hand he hid me;*
> *he made me into a polished arrow*
> *and concealed me in his quiver.* Isaiah 49:1-2

It is difficult to convey the impact this had on my life. In just two verses, God spoke volumes. I began to understand that he created me for a divine purpose. It had been established in heaven and now was being carried out here on earth. All of these struggles were for a purpose that God had planned before the creation of the universe. He knew me even then and set my life on his path.

"Before I was born the Lord called me." I knew the Lord had called me into his service. When I was seventeen years old, I felt the tug in my heart to follow Jesus with everything I had. I knew he would take me places I had not dreamed and use me beyond what I thought possible. But this was the first time that I realized all of this had been established before I was even born! I may have become aware of it when I was a young man, but the course of my life had been set in motion before I even came into existence. How wonderful it is to understand that God would love me so much that he would

predestine me for greatness in his kingdom. I certainly didn't feel very great while I was struggling in the trial of my crisis, but these things were about the future. I knew that my future had already been set for me. I took comfort in knowing that although I did not know where the future would lead me, God did. He not only knew, he had also planned it before I was born.

Names are very important to God. Throughout the Bible we read that God gave instruction to people about what to name their children. He told Abraham to name his son Isaac. He told Isaiah the prophet to name his son *Maher-Shalal-Hash-Baz*. That would seem to be an odd name. It means, 'quick to the plunder, swift to the spoil.' This name was important because it pointed to a prophecy Isaiah had spoken. God told Zechariah to name his son John, who would later be called John the Baptist. When Zechariah resisted, he was unable to speak until John's birth. Mary was told to name her son Jesus. These are a few of the times people were clearly instructed to give their children specific names.

"From my birth He has made mention of my name." God knows my name! I realized that I am not just another name to God. I have an identity that he created. He gave me my name before I was born. Long before my parents would give me my name, he had already given it to me. My name identifies me, my life, and my destiny. God may not have spoken directly to my parents specifically about my name, but when they were choosing, he certainly guided them to name me exactly what he had planned. I know that my name is just as important to God as any of the names in the Bible. A sense of importance came over me when I realized this. He is not only interested in me, I am also important to him!

"He made my mouth like a polished sword . . . he made me into a polished arrow." When I read this, it brought together exactly what God was communicating to me. You see, my name, *Barry*, means, 'spearlike; sharp or pointed.' He was telling me through these verses that

not only was I important, but my name is also who I am. It renewed
in me the call that I had felt many years ago when I was a teenager.
God had called me to speak, teach, preach, and now to write. When
I stripped away all the other things that seemed important to me,
the only thing left standing was this fact. I wasn't called to be rich or
famous. I wasn't called to work my whole life in a career as a lumber
distribution manager. I was called and set apart for a purpose. That
purpose is to teach people about God, his kingdom, and how to enter
into the full Christian life that he has reserved for all of us. I could
not escape this and I didn't want to. I was ready to surrender myself
to him and get on with my life within his will and purpose.

"[He has] *concealed me in his quiver."* There came to me that day
a deep realization that the best years of my life were ahead. The things
God had planned for me had not yet been tapped. Although I had
always known I was called and had been a pastor, the adventure of fulfilling God's will in my life still lay ahead. He had brought me to this
point in my life, used a crisis, and set me on the path that he had always
wanted for me. I would not fight it any longer. I was willing to forsake
all other dreams for the opportunity to realize my God-given destiny. It
became my passion and all other desires paled in comparison.

The purpose for my life had been renewed. I realized that this
time of despair and confusion in me was coming to an end. Although
the crisis was not over, it became much less important. I didn't have
to wake up every day and struggle just to make it through that day. I
didn't have to live under the weight of being unemployed. I had a new
purpose. With all I had within me, I was going to pursue what God
had planned. I didn't know where that would lead me, but I knew I
was entering in to a new time in my life. It would be a season of new
breakthroughs, a time when I would finally get down to the business
of fulfilling the wonderful calling that he had given. It would be a
place of honor, not in the eyes of men, but in the eyes and heart of the
One who had called me.

A New Desire

I had always heard phrases like, "having the mind of Christ," and "understanding God's will." I knew in theory what that meant, but I had never experienced any of these things. How could I know the mind of Christ? How could I really understand God's will for me? These were not questions that had easy answers. In fact, the answers didn't come just because I asked. The answers came when I began to live in the new call, purpose, and destiny God had for my life. As I began to really seek God and his will, I found that my mind began to be more like his. His will for my life began to be my desire. The more I desired the presence of God in my daily life, the more he revealed himself to me.

It was at this time that I happened to watch a movie entitled, *Gifted Hands.*[1] It is the true story of a man named Ben Carson. He was raised by a single mother. They struggled to make ends meet, and his mother worked constantly to attempt to provide a solid home for him and his brother. Ben got further and further behind in school and was in danger of failing. But his mother encouraged him to begin to read. It opened up a new world to him as he began to focus on his studies. He developed a drive to succeed. As he grew, he entered into a strong relationship with God and prayed regularly about his future.

Ben was able to secure a scholarship to Johns Hopkins School of Medicine. He excelled and soon was at the top of his class. Through all of this, he maintained his firm belief in God and his will for his life. He graduated and went on to become one of the leading neurosurgeons in the world. He successfully removed literally half of a young girl's brain to cure her of a lifelong disease. He later became the first surgeon in the world to successfully separate conjoined twins who shared vital organs. He is now a full professor of neurosurgery, oncology, plastic surgery, and pediatrics at Johns Hopkins.

It was not his successes that impressed me. It was his desire to be used by God to make a difference in the lives of others. He saw people through eyes of compassion and spent time praying for his patients. He asked God for the wisdom to know how to perform pioneering medical procedures. God did give him that wisdom. He was able to do what no other man had ever been able to do. This was accomplished not just by his talents, intellect, and abilities. It happened because he put God first and asked for his wisdom in the matters that faced him.

As I watched this, I began to weep. Soon I found myself on my knees crying out to the Lord. I asked him to help me to become a man like Ben. I cried over and over, "Lord, I just want to make a difference!" God had given Ben a calling and talent unlike any other person. And I knew that he had given me a different kind of call. It was one that dealt with the spiritual hearts of people, not their physical bodies. But my call was just as strong as Ben's. I wanted to pursue that with everything I had.

I heard an interview with Christian songwriter and performer, Stephen Curtis Chapman. He was discussing his life following the tragic accidental death of his five-year-old daughter. He described the incredible sorrow he and his family had endured. He talked about the grieving that took place. Many days he would wake up in the morning hoping that God had taken him to heaven so he could be with his daughter again. It was an emotional interview and I felt the impact of it. But his story did not end with the tragedy. He talked about the thousands of people who had heard the story and the effect it had on them. He had risen above the tragedy and asked God to help him touch others through the story of his family's crisis and their victory through it. Many have heard this story and given their lives to Jesus Christ as a result. The Chapmans decided that they would not live in the tragedy, but rather in the comforting and counseling of God. They turned a tragedy into a great victory for the kingdom of God.

Again, I was struck by the ability God has to take a crisis and turn it around for his glory. My struggle could not even compare to the tragedy the Chapmans had endured. But just as God had used that family to reach thousands because of their crisis, he would use mine to reach others with his grace, love and compassion. I understood it and all my desire was centered on that one thing. I wanted to make a difference in people's lives. God had given me substance through my struggle. He had rebuilt me, refocused me, and put a new desire in me to accomplish his will for my life no matter the cost.

SOME ENCOURAGEMENT FOR YOU

My prayer for you is that you will be able to understand that God intends to make your greatest defeat become your greatest victory. Through all of time, he has done just that in the lives of people. He took King David's defeat of sin and turned it into a great victory for the kingdom of heaven. David became a father in the line of Jesus himself. He used the apparent defeat of Jesus's death on the cross to become the greatest victory ever experienced by mankind. He defeated death and hell and established redemption for all who will enter in. He used the imprisonment of the great apostle Paul to encourage untold millions of people through his writings. This is who God is! You are not defeated. You are victorious! He is using your trial to perfect you and lead you into the destiny he has established for you. No longer see yourself as defeated because of your crisis. Rise up above the circumstance and boldly declare, "I am more than a conqueror through Christ who loved me!"

The past is over, the future is ahead. The present circumstance will also pass away. God is speaking to you about your future. Start seeing that this time is only a time of transition from the way you used to live to the new way you will live. If you are allowing God to make changes in your life and show you the victory that lies ahead, you will have your eyes on the future. It is an exciting place. It is a life of adventure. It is God's plan and will for you.

I have asked these questions of you already. I hope that by now you are able to answer. What is God's calling in your life? How can you make a difference for mankind? How can you make a difference for the kingdom of heaven? Every person has been given a specific mission in life. What is yours? You are not just another name to God. You were named by him and known by him before you even came into existence. You are incredibly equipped to fulfill his mission for your life. In fact, no one else on earth or in all of history could ever fulfill what God has ordained for you to accomplish. You are absolutely unique. There truly is no one else like you.

If you have trouble receiving this truth, ask God to give you a desire for his plan for your life. When you do that, you will see opportunities, not obstacles. Everything you experience will be another building block in the foundation God is laying in your life. You see, it has never been about just you. God is using your crisis to change the lives of others. He has been faithful to encourage you when you were grieving, counsel you when you needed help, and lead you when you needed direction. Now, look to the future! Look beyond the circumstance and see that his will for you is far greater than your crisis.

CONCLUSION

"FINISH STRONG"

A Lesson from Asaph

"But as for me, my feet had almost slipped;
I had nearly lost my foothold."

PSALM 73:2

A s I endured my time of crisis, there was a danger always lurking. If I would take my eyes off of God and begin to view my situation through my selfish nature, I found a place of despair and envy—yes, envy. This is the same issue that the Psalmist Asaph found himself facing. Although we don't know a great deal about him or the things he went through, he faced a crisis in his own life which he wrote about in Psalm 73. His crisis was one of faith. There was a time when he looked at others who did not spend the time he did following after God. In fact, these people he looked at were anything but God-followers. But there was an envy that rose up in Asaph's heart.

Asaph's observations about those who don't follow God were these: It appeared as if they had all the money and prosperity they wanted. It seemed like they were healthy and strong. None of the things that afflict common people seemed to apply to them. They boasted about their wealth and people went to them for help. They seemed to get richer and richer.

These observations led Asaph to doubt his place with God. You see, he had gone through his share of struggles, too. He wrestled to

147

understand why he was afflicted in many ways. He said that he had
been plagued and punished. Although he was careful not to accuse
God of doing this to him, it is clear that he had a very difficult circumstance or crisis that he was living in. His crisis got the better of
him for a time. Possibly for the first time in his life, Asaph felt that
following God and his plan may have all been for nothing.

*"Surely in vain have I kept my heart pure; in vain have I washed
my hands in innocence"* (Psalm 73:13). His circumstance became so
overwhelming that his endeavors to follow God seemed to be worth
nothing. After all, these wicked men were prospering in every way
while he struggled with affliction and anguish. What good was it to
invest in a relationship with God when these were the results? As he
tried to understand this it only led him into a deeper place of despair
and oppression.

But there was a turning point in Asaph's life. Something brought
him to his senses and made him understand that his life was not in vain.
His lifelong desire to seek after God was not a waste of time. In fact, it
was the most glorious of earthly endeavors. So what was it that changed
his mind? What led him to recant his conclusions about the wicked?

"I entered the sanctuary of God," he said in verse 17. In other words,
he went back to the place he had always lived, in God's presence. He
took his conclusions about the wicked, his observations of those who
didn't follow God, and placed them at the feet of God. When he
did that, all of his ideas were exposed for what they were—worldly
things. In the light of the presence of God, these things were nothing,
and Asaph saw them for what they really were. So he repented for the
thoughts that he had and his envy of wicked men. After he had done
this, he sang some of the most precious words about his God that
have ever been written:

> *Yet I am always with you;*
> *you hold me by my right hand.*

You guide me with your counsel,
and afterward you will take me into glory.
Whom have I in heaven but you?
And earth has nothing I desire besides you.
My flesh and my heart may fail,
but God is the strength of my heart
and my portion forever." Psalm 73:23-26

As I read these words, it summed up the struggle with my crisis. I had learned so many things from God. I had come so far with him. Why would I begin to envy those who live for the riches of the world? I could never lose track of the fact that everything I desired or longed for was found in my relationship with Jesus. I could not look at my circumstance and let it govern the way I felt. It could not dictate my days, my mood, or my life. I realized that I am found in God. He is the only reason for my life. Although the crisis was difficult, I must keep my eye on the prize. This prize is the all-surpassing knowledge that God is in absolute control of my life. I had come too far to fail now. So there rose up in me a resolve. I resolved to know nothing but Christ and him crucified. I resolved to continue my pursuit of God no matter the cost. He was the author of my life and all my desire was for him.

A young friend of mine wrote a song. Some of the lyrics found in it became a definition of the decision I had made. "Oh that I should lose it all, only to be found in You and for You to find me pleasing."[2] Complete dependence on God required this kind of commitment from me. Everything else paled in comparison to the overwhelming call I had answered to follow Christ and his will for my life.

FINISH STRONG

"I press on toward the goal to win the prize for which God
has called me heavenward in Christ Jesus."

PHILIPPIANS 3:14

Several months before I lost my job, a significant word from God came to me. At the time, I was a little confused by it, but as the months progressed and I entered my time of crisis, it began to make perfect sense. God's timing is always perfect and he had given me a foundation before I even faced my giant of a trial.

It came on a day when I was scheduled to teach a class at church. In my preparation for the lesson, the Lord spoke a clear word of direction into my life. He said, "Barry, finish strong!" My first reaction was: *Am I going to die soon? Is God telling me this because my days are short on the earth?* As I allowed the Holy Spirit to counsel me on the meaning of the direction, it became clear that I was not going to die. God was instructing me about the way he intended for me to live the rest of my life. I began to understand that these years of my life were to be the most productive, rich, and blessed I had ever experienced. My influence on my family, friends, and students would be more than ever before. I was to be solid.

Although I have never been much of a runner, I do know a few things about running a race. In distance racing, there are tactics that are used regularly. Most of these races are dictated for a time by the "pack." This is the group that includes virtually all of the runners. They spend as much as three quarters of the race running the same pace. This is intentional because it establishes the pace that all of the runners must attain to keep up. If a runner cannot attain this speed, he is said to "fall off the pace." He drops back and is no longer in contention to win. But there comes a point in the race when the pace quickens. The pack begins to dissipate and those who are the strongest begin to break away from the rest. At the preappointed time in the race, a runner "kicks." This means that he abandons the pace that has been set by others and runs with all his strength and speed toward the finish line. The one who is in the best physical condition and is able to run stronger and faster wins the race.

This was exactly what God was speaking to me. I had been in a spiritual race for all of my Christian life. I had run with the pack. I was moving closer to the finish line. Now, I was being challenged to kick. Philippians 3:14 meant more to me than it ever had before. I was to run for the rest of my life with the goal to not only finish, but to finish strong! I would now live my life to get the prize that God has waiting for me. I was not to get weaker and drop off the pace, but get stronger spiritually, follow the instructions God gives me, and run with passion for Him.

When I felt weak, the words were there, "finish strong." When I was overwhelmed by my crisis, they were still there, "finish strong." When I felt like I didn't understand the direction God was leading, it would come, "finish strong." When I felt hopeless, envious of others and defeated, "finish strong." God in his infinite grace and mercy had not only prepared me in advance for the struggle I would endure, but also gave me a solid lifelong goal. Finish strong!

An Overflowing Life

"Then I will teach transgressors Your ways,
and sinners will turn back to You."
PSALM 51:13

Earlier in this book I shared with you the powerful lessons David both learned and taught in Psalm 51. He went through a tremendous crisis in his own life. It was a crisis of his own doing. It involved great sin, yet ended in greater redemption. As a result of what David learned in regard to repentance, faith, forgiveness, love, mercy, and cleansing, he sang the powerful words of verse 13. He decided that what he had learned was so meaningful and powerful that he must share his story with everyone he saw.

I am convinced that every time David had a platform to speak or sing, he brought powerful testimony of God's faithfulness and love. He would tell of how he sinned and did not deserve the compassion of the Lord. Yet in his darkest hour, God was faithful to confront him in his sin and then lead him on a path of redemption that would be an example for all to follow. He knew that he had been given a great gift by a God who offered it through his great compassion and unfailing love. There were no options for David. He was compelled to speak of the great things God had done in his life.

Once again, I saw the truth of the Word come to life in me. I realized that I must do exactly what David did. He had been through a very dark time in his life, yet he gave glory to God, admitted his faults, and used that to teach others how to avoid the pitfall of sin. Even if others had committed sins that seemed unforgivable, he showed them that God was faithful to forgive them and cleanse them from the unrighteousness that follows sin. Likewise, I was going through a dark time in my life. Partially, it was of my own doing as well. Yet during this time, God had taught me life-changing things. He had placed in me a foundation that could not be shaken by anything that would come my way. I was forever changed and there was only one thing I could do—tell others about what had happened in my life.

The Lord showed me a picture of my life. I saw myself as a vessel. I imagined that it was like the ones that were at the wedding feast when Jesus changed their contents into fine wine for all the wedding guests. I saw it as a large clay or ceramic pot. It was flat at the bottom and got larger toward the middle. At the top, it narrowed again to the same diameter as the bottom. It stood about three feet tall. Then I saw this vessel being filled by water being poured in. The vessel filled to the brim. But the pouring did not stop. Water continued to flow into the pot. The only possible result was that the vessel overflowed. Water ran down the outside of it and covered the floor. Soon it touched other vessels as well. This is the picture of my life and relationship with God.

God began to reveal to me that the vessel is my life. The water being poured into me is the Holy Spirit revealing the things of the Lord to me. The one holding the pitcher that pours into me is God himself. As is always true of God, the pitcher never runs out of water. God continues to pour the things of the kingdom into my life through the water of the Holy Spirit. When I am continually filled, the only result is an overflow. I am a finite vessel, but the kingdom of God is infinite. Therefore, it must overflow.

God had certainly done this in my life in the time of trial. In spite of the difficult circumstance, in fact using the circumstance, he filled my spiritual life to overflowing. I could not contain all that he had done in me. The only thing left was to allow it to overflow and affect other vessels around me. You see, the vessel of my life does not stand alone. I am surrounded by family, friends, church members, neighbors, and a community. Other vessels stand around me. When the spiritual water overflows from my life, it touches those around me. In this way, I am able to reach out to others who are in need of what God has placed within me.

So I realized that the purpose for my crisis was ultimately not about me nearly as much as it was about those whom I would touch. Like David, I began to view my crisis and the spiritual victories that had occurred through it as spiritual water that could be used to encourage and help others. When I would teach, it was no longer just a matter of studying material and delivering the results to students. It became easy to simply share the things that God had done in me with others. I didn't have to study to learn about it, it was alive inside me. It had filled me up and could only overflow to those who needed the same things in their lives. This is the kind of spiritual water that far surpasses knowledge. It is not simply knowing about God and his Word, it is experiencing God and his Word. When that happened, I was free to allow the Holy Spirit to speak to others through the overflow from my life.

Some Final Words for You

I will make the rivers flow on barren heights,
and springs within the valleys.

I will turn the desert into pools of water,
and the parched ground into springs.
Isaiah 41:18

"[I will] *provide for those who grieve in Zion—*
to bestow on them a crown of beauty
  instead of ashes,
the oil of gladness
  instead of mourning,
and a garment of praise
  instead of a spirit of despair.
They will be called oaks of righteousness,
  a planting of the Lord
  for the display of his splendor.
Isaiah 61:3

You and I are on a journey. That journey has pinnacles and valleys. I have shared with you a deep valley in my life. Yet God did not leave me in that valley. He did not leave me to survive in a barren wilderness. He came and filled that valley with the water of the Holy Spirit. He turned a potentially dry and destructive place into a well-watered place filled with the beauty of new life that only comes from God. I can honestly say that the days of my crisis became the best days of my life with God. He changed me, built me, and brought life to dead places within me.

This is what God wants to accomplish through your time of crisis. His promise to you is this—he will not leave you there. Although you may not be out of the circumstance, you must know that it will pass. A new season of life awaits you. But in the meantime, he will fill your dry place, your desert, your valley with his water that brings life. While you are in a time of difficulty, drink in the pure spiritual water that God is offering you. Stop viewing your life as a desert and start seeing it as a spring of spiritual life welling up within you.

The result of doing this will be amazing! You will no longer mourn. You will no longer despair. You will no longer feel burned up by the desert heat. The impact of receiving the living water from God changes your life. You will not be tossed by circumstances, trials, or crises. You will be an "oak of righteousness, a planting of the Lord." His intent is to build you into an immovable, powerful son or daughter, one who is a subject of his kingdom.

Whether you are still in the midst of crisis or have emerged from one, God has a mission for you. First, don't be sidetracked by the ways of the world. Don't allow yourself to become envious of people who abound in worldly wealth, perfect health, and a trouble-free life. Instead, look to the "Author and Finisher" of your faith. The things that he is accomplishing in you are not earthly or carnal. They are eternal. As you allow God to fill you spiritually, this will overflow to your physical life as well. God's kingdom abounds in everything we need for life. Second, let God produce spiritual fruit in your life. No matter what your age, this is God's word to you: Make the days, months, and years that lay ahead the best of your life. Make them the most productive for the kingdom of God. Last and most importantly, tell your story! Allow God to fill you to overflowing and then simply allow that overflow to touch those around you. When that happens, not only has your life changed, but those who are touched are changed as well.

I have told my story. It is one that is yet to be completed. But I know that the things written in these pages are the overflow of God's incredible work in my life. He has forever changed me and the process continues. I hope you have read these words, taken them to heart, and allowed God to use your crisis to change your life for his glory. I made a decision to "draw near to God." This decision, made at the onset of my crisis, turned a devastating situation into an arena for victory. Make your own decision to draw near to God. Let Him change your life and your perspective. And then . . . *finish strong!*